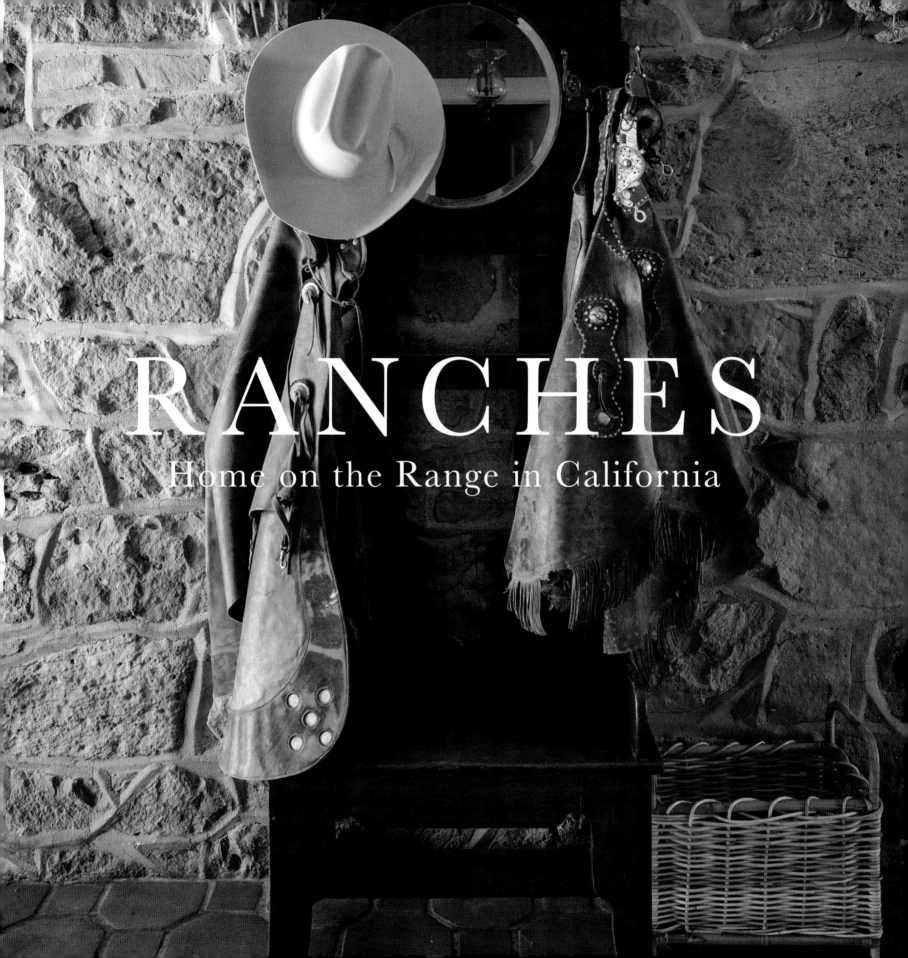

RANCHES

Home on the Range in California

RANCHES

Home on the Range in California

text by MARC APPLETON
photography by MELBA LEVICK

8.17.17 For Jane — Happy Trails!
Marc Appleton

RIZZOLI
NEW YORK

New York · Paris · London · Milan

To Uncle Jack, Aunt Lulamae, James and Helen
—M.A.

To my husband, Hugh, with love and gratitude
—M.L.

First published in the United States of America in 2016 by
RIZZOLI INTERNATIONAL PUBLICATIONS, INC.
300 Park Avenue South, New York, NY 10010
www.rizzoliusa.com

ISBN-13: 978-0-8478-4866-9
Library of Congress Control Number: 2016940433

Distributed to the U.S. Trade by Random House, New York

Front endpapers: Kathie Carlson and Sue Benech Field herding cattle at Hollister Ranch, Gaviota, California
Back endpapers: Main gate exit, Rancho Cienega del Gabilan, California
Page 1: Interior, Five Dot Ranch, Standish, California
Page 2: Piedra Blanca Ranch, San Simeon, California
Pages 4–5: Entry hall, French Ranch house, Thousand Oaks, California
Pages 6–7: Headquarters, Hunewill Ranch, Bridgeport, California

Designed by Douglas Curran

Printed and bound in China

2016 2017 2018 2019 2020 / 10 9 8 7 6 5 4 3 2 1

CONTENTS

INTRODUCTION

I have lived in or around big cities for most of my adult life, but when I drive out into the countryside on progressively smaller roads, through sparsely populated areas of open fields, pastures and farmland, I feel as if I am going home. The expansiveness of the landscape, the sounds of nature rather than man, even the smells appeal subliminally to my senses, and I remember. My wife tells me I'm the only person she knows who actually likes the smell of a skunk because it reminds me of my childhood.

I spent much of the 1950s and '60s growing up on three different ranches in Arizona. Long since a city slicker out of necessity and circumstance, I turned 70 last year, but the memories of a country life have never left my soul. When the publisher asked me to do this book with Melba Levick, the photographer, I didn't hesitate. I selfishly anticipated being able to travel down memory lane and indulge myself in rural excursions and experiences that had appealed mightily to me as a boy. In many respects, the journey has been that: researching, visiting various ranches, meeting and corresponding with ranch owners, managers and ranch hands have been nostalgically rewarding.

But it has also been a bittersweet experience: I've seen enough of the changes in California over the years to have been far more skeptical than my New York publisher, but even I had expectations that the California ranch was still alive and well, that cattle ranching, however marginalized by progress and suburban growth, was yet a viable and common enterprise, at least here and there throughout this great state. I discovered, sadly, that this was no longer the case.

We initially identified roughly 200 ranches. I am sure we overlooked some, but because we had limited space in the book, this was quickly reduced to about 125, and of those we eliminated 50 more "ranches" which hardly qualified for one reason or another, in many cases because neither livestock nor agriculture had ever been a vital part of their history. We began more focused research on the remaining 75, and in that process I came to more seriously doubt my original assumptions. In accepting the assignment, I had lobbied hard to do a book on *working* California ranches. I knew the publisher's interests did not incline towards pictures of the land, of cattle, horses or cowhands, but

PREVIOUS PAGES:
Elgin Hereford Ranch, Elgin, Arizona—the author's childhood home in the 1960s. Now an ecological research and conservation foundation.

OPPOSITE:
Pole hay barns, Likely Land & Livestock Ranch

were focused more on the architecture of the California ranch. In accepting all this, I still felt strongly that I could satisfy both of our expectations.

After months of further research and visiting many of the remaining 75 ranches, we reduced the number to 40 or so, and then finally to the 19 ranches we have included here. There were several attractive candidates that we wanted to include, but either we did not have space to do so or the owners declined. In their battle to survive financial, bureaucratic and environmental controls and obstacles, many ranchers have understandably developed an aversion to publicity and are not anxious to

be featured in the press or publications. Whether included or not, it was a privilege to consider them, and I learned from the research in the process.

So the book I first thought we might be able to do evolved and became a different one. In some respects, this was an inevitable outcome of today's reality: there are precious few working California ranches left in the state. Of the original Spanish and Mexican land grant ranches or *ranchos* that were from the first half of the nineteenth century and enduring into the twentieth, the historic backbone of the cattle ranching industry in California,

only a few remain. Most of the original adobe homesteads have disappeared or become vacant historic landmarks and museums. Many of the residual working ranches that do remain are also significantly smaller and have adopted grazing and land management practices that are more environmentally conscientious, but thereby also less productive. Add to this today's severe drought conditions, and it is no wonder that cattle ranching, at least in this state, appears to be nearing extinction.

There was a time when cattle ranching in California was the principal industry of the state, and the story began over 200 years after the Spanish conquest of

ABOVE:
Rancho Camulos, Piru. The main adobe and south porch were the setting for Ramona.

OPPOSITE:
School bell, Rancho Camulos

the Americas and their establishment in 1535 of the vice-royalty of New Spain in what is now Mexico. In an effort to extend their territorial domination north into what was called *Alta California*, Spanish Catholic priests of the Franciscan order began establishing a chain of missions to convert existing indiginous populations into the faith. The first and southernmost, Mission San Diego de Alacà, was established in 1769, and the northernmost, San Francisco Solano, in 1823. Stretching from San Diego to the southern end of the Napa Valley, a total of 21 missions and several presidios became New Spain's primary religious and military outposts along what was called the Camino Real—(the Royal or King's Road). The missions began livestock grazing as well as farming on the surrounding lands. The story of the great ranchos, which were ultimately to become the first major private real estate holdings in California, was preceded by the establishment of these missions.

Spanish rule—as remote as it was from its principal seat—would not endure, and it was challenged in 1810 by separatists, during the Mexican War of Independence, who in 1822 finally succeeded in taking over the Spanish territories. Mexico's Colonization Act of 1824 and its supplementary *Regalmento* of 1828, making it easier to obtain land grants, were enacted to further promote

agricultural development, liberalize trade and encourage settlement in Alta California. In 1829, ironically long before the U.S. was to do so, slavery was officially abolished, incentivized by Mexico's renunciation in 1924 of the Spanish cast system. As the newly independent Mexican Republic matured, there were increasing demands for the secularization or "disestablishment" of the missions, and in 1833 the Mexican Congress passed an act officially secularizing the mission properties. Interested in colonizing Alta California, rewarding loyalists and enriching the new government's coffers, the republic divided and sold many of the mission properties over the next several decades as land grants to private individuals and families. Thus was born the great network of several hundred ranchos which for many years dominated the state and which to this day are a defining factor in California real estate.

The ranchos were generally granted by political favoritism principally to Mexican loyalists, but some were also acquired by enterprising U.S. citizens who, by immigrating under the Colonization Act and agreeing to become citizens of the new Mexican Republic, had been able to petition for and purchase land grants. A few had already received grants for grazing permits under Spanish rule, and the new government honored many of these follow-

Piedra Blanca Rancho, San Simeon

ing reviews of title. The new republic, however, was an unsteady and somewhat disorganized government torn by civil strife, and when a greedy United States annexed Texas in 1846, it led to a larger conflict between the two countries—The Mexican–American War—not just over Texas but a number of other states including the western terri-

tories of New Mexico, Arizona, Utah, Nevada, Colorado and California. Mexico proved no match for the U.S. forces, and the war soon ended with the Treaty of Guadalupe Hidalgo in 1848 by which California, along with the other contested areas, were ceded to the U.S. In 1850, California officially became a state.

*Water tower, bunkhouse and
adobe ranch house,
Rancho Santa Margarita*

Some of the original grantees of the ranchos retained their holdings and prospered, but the majority would lose out to more aggressive Anglos, some of whom literally stole properties by taking advantage of the 1852 Land Commission process. Along with America's belief in Manifest Destiny, the Gold Rush of 1948, and later incentivization from the Homestead Act of 1862, a significant migration westward had started to affect California's economy. Cattle ranching was expanding exponentially to meet the growing markets for hides, tallow and, eventually, beef.

In the 1860s, however, an economic recession and drought followed by record rains and flooding, and then more drought, would cripple smaller and borderline ranchers, making them easier targets for wealthy entrepreneurs. The latter part of the nineteenth century saw the rise of "industrial cowboys," cattle barons like Henry Miller and his partner Charles Lux, who on the backs of Gold Rushers rose from running butcher shops to owning more land and cattle and controlling more water rights than anyone else in California. The indigenous tribes, which had essentially gone from religious

slavery during the mission era to commercial servitude on the ranchos, had suffered most from all this, but now even many of the original land grantees were forced in turn to sell their rancho lands to more enterprising white settlers. As Robert Cleland colorfully described it in his book *The Cattle on a Thousand Hills*,

> The wealth, culture, and civilization of the East were preparing to engulf the land; and the pioneer days of southern California were slipping into the irrecoverable past as fast as the waters of a mountain stream sink into the dry sands of the Mojave Dessert.

The California ranch evolved into the twentieth century but would be further reduced by competition from other industries and interests, including the huge feedlots of the Midwest, as well as the demand locally for real estate for suburban growth. The great rancho, once the icon of the state's industrial strength, was no longer a dominant force. In recent decades, many remaining family ranchers and farmers have sold to real estate speculators, developers, or wealthy city folks looking for "a place in the country." These sales often signal a reduction or cessation of ranching and farming activities.

While more favorable ranching conditions have continued in other states, Cali-

fornia cattle ranchers have faced a competitive beef market, drought conditions and environmental restrictions, and have struggled over the last several decades to develop range management practices that better respect the land. Where once the expansive wilderness offered the pioneers a free, plentiful and seemingly endless source of grassland to be consumed and trampled, California's real estate eventually became far too valuable for such careless use. Most cattle ranches, now significantly more limited in acreage, could not afford to support large herds while sustaining a healthy renewable range environment. The arid western climate compounded the situation in offering up more fragile vegetation. *Home on the Range*, the song once considered the unofficial anthem of the West, could no longer claim "seldom was heard a discouraging word."

Recently, holistic or biodynamic agriculture has been increasingly promoted, where a suitable balance between livestock grazing and environmental sustainability are of greater concern. The feedlot operation, although it is still the largest (albeit least advertised) way of raising beef in the U.S., has been deemed by many critics to be a qualitatively suspect operation. It is troubled by the use of antibiotics and growth hormones, resulting in more rapid growth but lower quality and less healthy meat, not to mention the chemicals typically used to break down the thousands of tons of concentrated urine and manure waste that feed lots produce. Among California ranches there has been an increasing tendency towards more sustainable rangeland management with rotational grass-fed grazing of reduced numbers of cattle, but the market for higher-priced "organic" beef is limited and not that profitable for many ranchers. Some who are fearful of losing their ranches to development have also taken steps to partner with environmental groups like Nature Conservancy or create permanent easements through organizations like the California Rangeland Trust that will prevent subdivision and help protect ranch environments. Commercial ranching today, at least in California, is a very different and threatened proposition.

A 2015 report by the World Health Organization also does not bode well for the meat industry, promoting instead a plant based diet, and highlighting the risk red meat—and particularly processed meats—raises for cancer and heart disease. The current research and meat alternatives—healthy vegetable-based substitutes that taste like real beef—will likely be a further challenge to ranchers and the beef industry. Joseph D. Puglisi, a Stanford University professor of structural biology, is an advisor to Beyond Meat, a startup in this new arena with significant business backing. Beyond Meat's founder, Ethan Brown, was apparently inspired when he read that livestock was the cause of more greenhouse gases than the entire transportation industry. Whether this statistic was true or not, the company's growth—with products in 360 stores in 2013 to over 7,500 stores in 2015, and soon to include Walmarts—has been impressive, although it may still be a challenge to convert the diets of most meat-loving Americans.

The book, which evolved from our original search for working ranches, has inevitably taken a wider view. It is to some extent a glimpse into the birth, growth and eventual decline of cattle ranching in California, the romance which has attended that story, and the courageous few ranchers who are still struggling to preserve a way of life and an environment that has been an integral part of western America's history. For these few, that romance assumes a grittier and more pragmatic reality. The book is not just about the diminished state and environment of working California ranches, but the architecture of their ranch houses, barns, outbuildings, fences and equipment. In these images one can appreciate the rusted, worn and faded condition of a way of life that is disappearing. In some cases, the architecture is still occupied and lovingly cared for, maintained by subsequent generations of the original

Porch, main house,
Joel McCrea Ranch,
Thousand Oaks

families or by new owners. In others, the buildings reflect the reality of the gradual decline of the California ranch and have become the symbolic ruins of a once thriving enterprise.

Oddly, the realization that the book would have to have a different emphasis gave new meaning to our project. In a sense, we would be documenting the passing of a way of life and the places where it had once prospered. We realized that a book on California ranches would have to acknowledge this loss and accept more than just working cattle ranches. It would not so much be about California ranches as about what has *happened* to California ranches. Yes, it would include working ranches, but it would also include historic ranchos now museums, and ranches that, in order to preserve their scenic environment, have evolved and transformed to include planned developments and enterprises other than raising livestock. It would even include some that had been purchased and developed by the well to-do as subsidized retreats for their private use. Into this last category fell the "trophy," "celebrity" or "gentleman's" ranches which, although in some cases they were actually working ranches, were also romantic recreations by wealthy or famous folks of a life outside the cities in which their fame and fortunes had often been made.

Related to all this is the premise that for most of us our common presumptions about the western ranch have evolved from an idealized rather than real lifestyle. We have for at least a couple of centuries certainly admired and idolized the image of the fictional cowboy— whether on the page or screen. This appreciation is a highly edited one: as we know from a more careful reading of western history, the uglier aspects of human nature and behavior were often left out of that appreciation. Just as the cowboy gradually became an idealized figure romanticized in literature by authors like Owen Wister, Zane Grey and Will James, depicted by artists like Frederick Remington, Charles Russell and Edward Borein, and finally memorialized in films by Hollywood, so too the cattle ranch became to some degree a mythical creation, something imagined more than actually experienced by most Americans.

However idealized in our national psyche, it could still be argued that the values and lessons learned from ranch life have traditionally been more constructive than most urban experiences, and so perhaps understandably the legend persists. The character traits of the fictionalized cowboy do indeed have a foundation in ranching. We can discount the myth, but we must recognize and appreciate the character, and that character is one still shared by many working ranchers.

I am in sympathy with those ranchers who try to hold on to something to which they and their ancestors were devoted and took for granted. I admire their stubbornness against the odds. If I could choose a companion to ride with into the unknown, give me the rancher any day over the professor, banker, politician, lawyer, or architect. Perhaps in my case this is partly sentimental nostalgia, but I believe the rancher to be generally tougher, more observant and less complaining company. By the same token the California ranch may be a much reduced, oppressed and battered version of its former self, but it still merits our attention—before it is gone forever.

HISTORIC RANCHES

RANCHO CAMULOS

PIRU, CALIFORNIA
1842

Rancho Camulos, currently the only National Historic Landmark in Ventura County, is perhaps best known as the purported home of Ramona, Helen Hunt Jackson's fictional heroine from her romantic 1884 novel *Ramona*, the publication of which may have done more to spread the mythic cultural identity of Southern California than almost any other event. The book had more than 300 printings and spawned five films beginning with D.W. Griffith's of 1910, starring Mary Pickford and shot at Rancho Camulos. As Harriet Beecher Stowe's Uncle Tom's Cabin had done for African American culture in the eastern states, *Ramona* encouraged a sympathetic view of Hispanic culture in the western states and an acceptance of racial diversity.

Rancho Camulos, however, had its true beginnings as part of a larger 48,612-acre holding called Rancho San Francisco, granted in 1839 to Antonio del Valle, the administrator for the Mission San Fernando, which had been at-tempting to convert the Tatavian Indian tribe, which was native to the area. Part of this tribe lived in a village called *Kamulus* at the western edge of the rancho. On Antonio del Valle's death in 1841, the land was divided among the del Valle family members, and one of Antonio's sons, Ygnacio del Valle, estab-lished a cattle ranch in 1842 in this western section called Camulos. In 1853, not far from the Santa Clara River, he built for his foreman the first four rooms of what eventually would become the main adobe.

Ygnacio, his second wife Ysabel and their children were then living in Los Angeles, but in 1861 they moved per-manently to Rancho Camulos. They added three new rooms and a basement to the adobe for their growing family, which by 1870 numbered 12 children. While drought conditions in the 1860s forced his del Valle siblings to sell most of the larger Rancho San Francisco, Ygnacio and his family managed to prosper. When Ygnacio died in 1880,

LEFT: *The 1930 school house*
ABOVE: *Interior stair at the main adobe*

FOLLOWING PAGES: *Porch of the* cocina *or kitchen wing; the vine is solandra maxima ("cup of gold")*

the number of cattle had expanded significantly, and the ranch included agricultural farming of fruit trees, grape vineyards, and other crops. After a time, ranch operations supported a population of approximately 200 Mexican and Indian employees, and the adobe had expanded to 20 rooms with numerous accessory buildings, including a brick winery, barn, chapel and employee housing. The building of the winery in 1867 signaled an expansion of the vineyard, and by 1870 the production from 90,000 pounds of grapes of 6,000 gallons of wine and 800 gallons of brandy, made Rancho Camulos one of the largest producers in the county. In 1908 the del Valle family incorporated the ranch as the del Valle Company, but disagreements among the heirs, followed by the death of several family members, led to the sale of the ranch in 1924, and an end to its Hispanic heritage.

Charles Lummis, the esteemed historian, editor, librarian, journalist, Indian rights activist and preservationist, was a frequent visitor to Rancho Camulos and friend of the del Valle family. When he failed to convince the State of California to purchase the ranch as a historic park, he wrote:

> It has been 40 years since I first visited Camulos. Since that time, it has been like my own home, and its people like my own. The old folks were like parents to me. The romance, the traditions, the customs of Camulos are all familiar and dear to me—not merely because they are Camulos, but because that was the last stand of the patriarchal life of Spanish California, which has been so beautiful to the world for more than a century.

The new buyer of the property was August Rubël, the son of a Swiss immigrant father and American mother, who had grown up in New York and who was a graduate of Harvard College. At the age of 23 and newly arrived to Ventura County with his wife Mary, he had dreams of owning a ranch and raising a family in a bucolic setting. The Rubël family tenure became another chapter altogether in the history of the ranch. Rubël made a few changes, among them the addition in 1930 of a schoolhouse, where the family's five children along with his bookkeeper's children were schooled, and increasing the citrus and agricultural crops. He was nevertheless a conscientious steward of the heritage he had acquired, and preserved in the old winery many artifacts from the past and, on occasion, opened Rancho Camulos to visitors and local school groups. He was killed in Tunisia in 1943 during World War II, however, and three years later his widow remarried

The altar of the 1867 chapel, which also has a large open air porch to accommodate a larger congregation.

Edwin Burger, who following her death in 1968 maintained the ranch but was far less accommodating of visitors.

When Burger died in 1994, the Rubël children, who revered their father's memory, took back the ranch. They and their children continued the citrus farming on the majority of the ranch's re-maining 1,800 acres, but the 1994 Northridge Earthquake had caused serious damage to some of the buildings, particularly the brick winery, and the cost of repairing the damage was challenging. In 1996, generously assisted by Ventura County historic preservationists and board members from the Ventura County Museum, the Rubël family was

RIGHT: *To the left, beyond the lemon tree, is the grape arbor.*

BELOW: *JY del Valle serveying Camulos Rancho. Photo courtesy of Seaver Center for Western History Research, Los Angeles County Museum of Natural History.*

successful in having the ranch listed on the National Register of Historic Places, and in 2000 the buildings and 40 acres were designated a National Historic Landmark, assuring their survival. Funds were raised to begin repairing some of the buildings, and the non-profit Rancho Camulos Museum now caretakes the property, which is open to the public.

OPPOSITE:
Citrus-picking platform

RIGHT:
*The ranch gas station,
ca. 1910.*

There are vestiges of a rich past at Rancho Camulos, but like many historic California ranchos, its active life as a family ranch has disappeared. From Highway 126 between Santa Paula and Santa Clarita, there are still signs of productive agricultural activity in the many fields and orchards in the valley, and the typical suburban sprawl that has covered much of Ventura County has not yet severely impacted the area. Today, however, as the traffic speeds by no more than a stone's-throw from Rancho Camulos, the ranch's main buildings go unnoticed by most travelers and seem merely part of the aging agricultural scenery. For those who take the time to pull off the highway, perhaps distracted by the discreet historic marker on the side of the road, a rare and rewarding glimpse into a part of California's history awaits them.

RANCHO SANTA MARGARITA

SANTA MARGARITA, CALIFORNIA
1841

The Santa Margarita Ranch is located just east of Route 101 between Atascadero and San Luis Obispo. You can see part of it from the highway, its main buildings raised slightly on the hills, which once provided a vantage point surveying the surrounding scenery.

The Mission San Luis Obispo de Tolosa to the south was founded by Spanish Franciscan missionaries in 1772. Fifteen years later an "assistant" mission was formally established to the north on the Camino Real, the historic trail connecting California's 21 missions. Called Santa Margarita de Cortona Asistencia, it was located in territory that was purportedly occupied by the Salinan and Chumash Indian tribes. Around 1787, the missionaries established the *asistencia*, and eventually, about 1817, a large stone structure was built to accommodate lodging, a chapel, grainery and related farm storage. It was allegedly one of the first uses of mortared masonry construction in California. Today the archaeological remnants of this structure are still visible inside a wooden barn exterior, constructed much later.

After Mexico secured its independence from Spain in 1822, the mission properties throughout California were privatized. In 1841, 17,735 acres of ranch land, including the asistencia, were granted to Joaquin Estrada, whose half-brother Juan Bautista Alvardo was Governor of Alta California, and who apparently loved to entertain at Santa Margarita with fiestas and rodeos. Following the severe drought of 1860 and facing significant financial debt, however, he was forced to sell the ranch in 1861 to Martin Murphy Jr. Murphy and his wife Mary immediately turned the management of the ranch over to their 21-year-old son Patrick, a general in the California National Guard. Patrick Murphy soon expanded cattle operations to include 61,000 acres of adjacent Rancho Atascadero and Rancho Asuncion and in 1876 he also purchased Rancho Cojo, an additional 9,000 acres.

Part of the Rancho Santa Margarita herd

During his tenure, Patrick Murphy added wood clapboard siding and Victorian era details to the original Estrada adobe house. A structure called the Wells Fargo building just west of the adobe apparently functioned as a general store and stagecoach stop. In 1889, Murphy managed to convince the Southern Pacific Railroad, to whom he offered a right of way, to come through the ranch, and soon a small town grew up around the station. Today the town of Santa Margarita with a current population of about 1,300 is still surrounded by the Santa Margarita Ranch. Murphy died in 1901, and in 1904 his heirs sold the ranch to three brothers—Ferdinand, Christian and Gustav Reis—Germans who had emigrated west with the Gold Rush.

The Reis brothers began extensive modifications to the ruins of the asistencia related to their ranch operations. The ranch remained in the Reis family until 1969, when it was willed to Stanford University, which then sold it in 1975 to the Robertson family of Texas. The Robertsons operated the ranch until 1998, when the ranch holdings of about 16,000 acres were purchased by a partnership among Doug Fillipponi, Karl

Whittstrom and Rob Rossi. Fillipponi and Whittstrom oversee a grass-fed livestock operation of approximately 700 cow-calf pairs of Black Angus cattle. Like many ranches these days, the cattle operation consists of rotational grazing and sustainable rangeland management practices. Rossi, the third partner, who owns the headquarters, attends to other ranch developments, which now include hosting a variety of public and private events—weddings, social gatherings, festivals and fundraisers. In an effort to encourage tourism, the original adobe now houses a small museum, a two-mile loop narrow gauge Pacific Coast Rail-

road circling the property has been added, there's a zip line, and the ranch partners with several outside commercial enterprises. There is also a 1,000-acre vineyard on the ranch, and Rossi and his partners are in the process of developing a housing project of approximately 100 homes (Margarita Vineyard Estates).

These new developments run the risk of overshadowing cattle ranching, but since it is no longer as financially feasible that traditional cattle ranching can be the sole support, particularly in areas of California that are now se-

LEFT:
Original adobe to the left, bunkhouses and water tower

ABOVE:
The newer barn, constructed in 1998 in corrugated metal to protect the original stone asistencia ruins. Exterior wood siding was added more recently over the corrugated metal.

*The original adobe
ranch house, with
added late nineteenth-
century Victorian porch,
siding and details*

verely affected by drought conditions,
the development of alternative sources
of revenue such as these at Santa Margarita Ranch are now more common,
and at least allow the prospect that portions of the original ranch environment
and its historical buildings may survive.
Subdivision and development in the
surrounding areas of San Luis Obispo
County are now prevalent. One might
stop short of calling Santa Margarita
Ranch's programs eco-tourism, but the
ranch is clearly striving in its own fash-
ion to at least partly preserve key ele-
ments of its heritage and to share them
with the public.

ABOVE AND LEFT:
Newer asistencia barn

FOLLOWING PAGES:
Narrow gage railroad

RANCHO LOS ALAMITOS

LONG BEACH, CALIFORNIA

1833

In the middle of the suburban sprawl that has grown up around the community of Long Beach, it is surprising to come upon a partial vestige of a more rural past that has so far withstood urban pressures. Even though its once expansive land holdings have been reduced to only 7.5 acres occupying a small hilltop, the landscape at Rancho Los Alamitos ("Ranch of the Little Cottonwoods") tells a rich story possibly dating back to 500 A.D.

Once the site of the ancestral village of Povuu'ngna of the indigenous Gabrielino-Tongva people, and still a valued site for them today, in 1790 the land became part of Los Coyotes— 300,000 acres awarded to Manuel Nieto by the Spanish Crown for his service on the Gaspar de Portolá expedition. Nieto died in 1804, purportedly the wealthiest man in California.

Sometime between 1804 and 1833, a hilltop adobe was built for Nieto's vaqueros and their horses on a section of land called Alamitos. Upon subdividing Los Coyotes into five great ranchos in 1833, Juan José Nieto, the oldest son, sold Rancho Los Alamitos to Governor José Figueroa who established a company with the intent of stocking the 28,500-acre ranch. In 1834 Figueroa died and his brother took over the property, runing it until 1842, when it was acquired by Abel Stearns.

Stearns became a wealthy, powerful man, but in the early 1860s, crippling droughts followed by record rains and floods were devastating. He borrowed from San Francisco financier Michael Reese using Alamitos as collateral, defaulted, and in 1866, Reese took title. Reese leased out his ranch, and in 1878, John Bixby, cousin to the owners of Rancho Los Cerritos, and his wife, subleased and moved into the old adobe. By 1881, the entire ranch was offered for sale. In partnership, John Bixby, J. Bixby & Company and Isaias Hellman bought Alamitos.

The main ranch house, framed by an old California pepper tree (left) and Morton Bay fig tree (right)

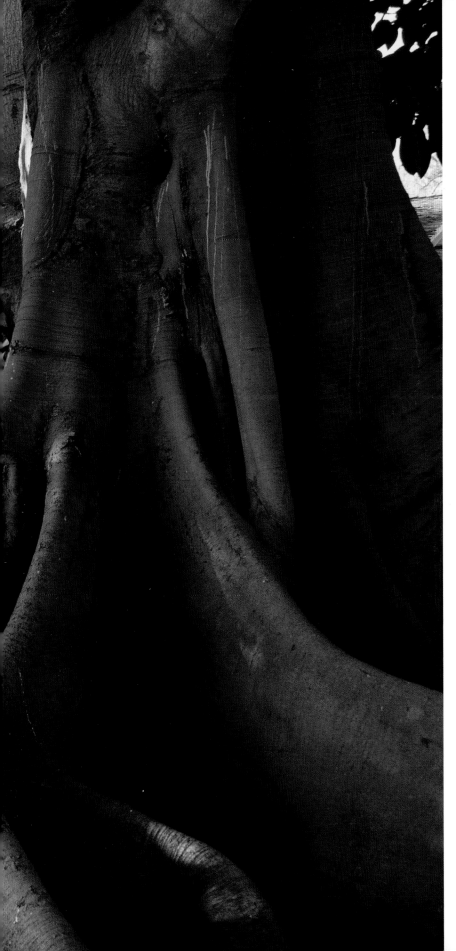

LEFT: *The ranch house porch, seen over the massive roots of the Morton Bay fig tree (Ficus Macrophylla) planted ca. 1890*

ABOVE: *A "San Diego" bougainvillea vine covers a corner of the ranch house (top); cowboy office sign (bottom)*

RIGHT: *Front porch interior with rattan furniture. The Della Robbia–style plaque at the end was acquired by Florence Bixby on a 1926 trip to Europe.*

FOLLOWING PAGES: *Back hallway opening into the main hall of the adobe portion of the house*

The Bixby family and their descendants thus began a long and prosperous commitment to Rancho Los Alamitos which has lasted to the present day. The original ranch, however, has gone through significant changes. During the real estate boom of the 1880s, portions of the ranch started to be developed and following John Bixby's death in 1887, his widow Susan inherited only the heart of the rancho.

Despite her efforts to shift her son's, Fred Bixby's, horizons away from Long Beach and toward the wider cosmopolitan world, Fred and his new bride, Florence, returned in 1898 to the ranch, where they were to make it their permanent home. They expanded the ranch's compound of buildings, and in the 1920s with the discovery of oil on Signal Hill and Seal Beach, the family fortunes grew significantly. Over the years Florence enlisted several eminent landscape designers, including Paul Howard, Florence Yoch and the Olmsted Brothers under her confident direction to help develop

the extensive gardens which were to become a unique signature of the ranch.

After a long and rewarding life and years of devotion to Rancho Los Alamitos, but faced with the likely prospect that what was left of the ranch headquarters might not survive future generations, the family donated the ranch to the City of Long Beach, preserving its remarkable heritage. Today the ranch is a public-private venture with Rancho Los Alamitos Foundation, open to visitors, and the host of an active program of educational events.

ABOVE:
"Bristol," a half-breed shire draft horse

OPPOSITE:
The billiard room, main ranch house

LEFT:
Feed shed and corrals shaded by California pepper trees

FOLLOWING PAGES:
Back patio courtyard. Among four small Pygmy date palms is a large beaucarnea (right rear)—all planted ca. 1923.

WORKING
RANCHES

RANCHO CIENEGA DEL GABILAN

HOLLISTER, CALIFORNIA
1843

Rancho Cienega del Gabilan (Wetlands of the Hawk) is picturesquely situated in the Gabilan Mountain Range near what is now the town of Hollister. It was first inhabited by the Matsun tribe, members of the Ohlone people. When the Spanish claimed the land, and the Mission San Juan Bautista was established in 1797, cattle were first introduced to the area. Following the secularization of the missions by the new Mexican republic, the ranch land became part of a land grant to Antonio Chaves in 1843, who served as tax collector as well as a senior lieutenant in Mexico's military.

Chavez's tenure on the ranch did not last long. The influx of U.S. immigrants to the Sacramento Valley had already begun by the 1840s. In 1846, Colonel John C. Fremont entered the capital city of nearby Monterey, and from there moved his small army to Gabilan where they further threatened Mexican forces. Although open warfare between the two nations was for the moment avoided, these confrontations set the stage for the short-lived Bear Flag Revolt in June and July of 1846, which was soon followed that same year by the U.S.'s occupation of California and its ultimate takeover in 1848.

Wounded in one of the skirmishes, Chaves fled to Mexico and reputedly transferred title to Rancho Cienega del Gabilan to Jose Y. Limantour. Limantour, who had suspiciously acquired a number of land grants during this volatile period, spent a decade unsuccessfully defending his claims, and in 1857 he granted an equally suspect quitclaim for the rancho to U.S. Consulate Thomas O. Larkin. When Larkin died in 1858, Jesse D. Carr purchased the rancho and spent the better part of the next decade clearing an admittedly confusing and convoluted chain of title. Still standing today is the original ranch house Carr built in 1867.

Through the end of the nineteenth century and into the twentieth, the ranch

ABOVE: *Cienega del Gabilan, 1867 ranch house. From* East of the Gabilans, *pg. 58.*

LEFT:
The ranch house today

RIGHT:
Living room, ranch house

BELOW:
A boot-lined stairway, ranch house

along with adjacent acreage was sold and purchased numerous times. In 1907, John S. Bryan, who had coincidentally married Jessie Carr, the senior Carr's daughter, purchased 8,571 acres of the ranch land. When Bryan died the land passed to his widow, and she sold it in 1928 to Lawrence A. Kelly, who added 771 acres to the ranch before selling it only a year later to Rollin Reeves, who added another 1,000 acres.

LEFT:
The old Glenwood kitchen stove

OPPOSITE:
Desk and family memorabilia

A bedroom, ranch house

The Reeves family and their offspring have held the ranch, currently 11,190 acres, in their family ever since, maintaining a working cattle operation, but also proving to be conscientious stewards of the ranch environment. Over the years the older ranch buildings have been maintained and several new buildings have been added. The clan has grown through three generations to become the Reeves-Baldocchi-Boyle families, which today operate the ranch as the Gabilan Cattle Company. A working cow-calf operation, some 20 family members are still involved in the business and day to day challenges, dedicated to maintaining their heritage and the land they love. Sustaining a holistic and more conscientious cattle operation sensitive to the environment is never easy, particularly during times of severe drought, but they have partnered with the Nature Conservancy in an effort to insure that the land will never be developed.

ABOVE:
Prized bull (top); improvised door bolt
made from horseshoes (bottom)

RIGHT:
The barn

ABOVE:
A well worn saddle

RIGHT:
Julie Baldocchi, with her son and one of the ranch hands

HUNEWILL RANCH

BRIDGEPORT, CALIFORNIA
1861

Napoleon Bonaparte Hunewill was born in 1828 in Maine. He came to California during the Gold Rush, made a small fortune, then returned to Maine, where in 1859 he married a childhood neighbor, Esther Ann Hughes. Napoleon returned to California with his bride and her brother and his wife, reaching San Francisco in 1860, and began operating a sawmill. When the sawmill was destroyed by floodwaters in 1861, they headed east to the town of Aurora with a mining venture in mind. Instead of mining, they decided instead to start another sawmill, this time in Big Meadows near Bridgeport, east of what is now Yosemite National Park, where Napoleon filed for water rights (1861) and a homestead (1862).

By 1872, the family had acquired sufficient land to start a cattle operation, and by the early 1880s had built the barn and main Victorian style ranch house, both of which survive to this day. In 1883, their son, Frank, who had attended U.C. Berkeley, became an attorney and married Alice Hyde, and the couple returned to live at the ranch. With the next generation of the Hunewill family, grandson Stanley eventually took over management of the ranch following the death of Napoleon in 1908. That same year he formed the Hunewill Land & Livestock Company and began raising prize Hereford cattle and registered Morgan horses. Stanley married in 1915 and had three children before the marriage ended in divorce. He remarried Lenore Martin in 1928. The older children, their son Stan and the grandchildren have continued to support the family corporation and manage the ranch.

By 1931 and with the Depression, Stanley and Lenore had started to take in guests at the ranch as a source of additional income. Today, while managing some 1,200 head of cattle and 190 horses, the family carries on the guest ranch hospitality. Like similar ranches, many of the guests look forward to participating in the seasonal cattle drives and ranch work in a setting that remains some of the most spectacular scenery California has to offer.

The white Victorian ranch house

BELOW: *An old piano occupies a corner of a room in the ranch house (top); young boys driving donkeys on Hunewill Ranch. Photo courtesy of Hunewill Ranch (bottom).*

RIGHT: *The Victorian style ranch house from the 1880s, with its elegantly detailed porch and clapboard "quoins" at the building's corners*

PREVIOUS PAGES: *Barn, with cattle egrets on ridge*

ABOVE: *Saw mill blades*
LEFT: *An old buckboard wagon*

A pair of guest ranch horses

LIKELY LAND & LIVESTOCK RANCH

LIKELY, CALIFORNIA
1871

Route 395, the famous scenic highway in eastern California, meanders north from Los Angeles between Death Valley and the Eastern Sierras, past Yosemite and Lake Tahoe all the way to Oregon. About 100 miles east of Mount Shasta in the County of Modoc, it runs through the little town of Likely (population 200). In the 1840s, General John Fremont and his guide Kit Carson had explored the area, which was occupied by the Native Pit Indians. It was here in the valley of the South Fork of the Pit River that John D. Flournoy, who had emigrated west in 1845 from Missouri and worked as a cowhand in Yolo County near Sacramento, settled in 1871 and began ranching. In 1878 he married his wife, Mary, and started a family.

Today, John's three great grandsons—Bill, John and David—and their families continue the enterprise. In 1973 they formed the Likely Land & Livestock Company as a partnership with their father, Don. The ranch is a commercial beef operation that supports a herd of approximate 2,500 cows, 500 heifers and 100 bulls on 18,000 deeded acres plus additional Federal, BLM and Forest Service leases for summer grazing. Approximately 3,000 acres are devoted to agricultural production of several thousand tons of hay each year.

The brothers have each taken on different duties in running the ranch. Bill is married to Athena and is primarily responsible for the cattle operation; John, married to Sydney, oversees water, irrigation and the agricultural fields; and Dave, married to Joanne, is the mechanic responsible for the ranch vehicles and equipment. It is very much a family affair, where the division of responsibilities is mutually supportive.

The ranch, which includes a portion of the South Fork of the Pit River, is fortunate to have fairly plentiful amounts of both spring and well water. In grading and developing the hay fields, the South Fork, previously channeled and

The Flournoy family compound, including the separate cook-house, where the brothers and their families meet for breakfast to discuss the day's tasks.

then its channels overrun, had become a source of significant erosion, but the Flournoys have worked conscientiously with the Central Modoc Resource Conservation District, the Regional Water Quality Control Board and others to correct the problems.

In 1997, noticing that its purebred Angus bulls and cows were producing calves that were decreasing in vigor, reproduction and longevity, the ranch joined a program called the Harris Ranch Partnership for Quality. The program—a Heterosis Project conducted to study the beneficial effects of crossbreeding to enhance productivity—has led to changes at the ranch, which now involve the crossbreeding of Hereford bulls with Angus cows, with positive results. Bill has also been especially active in the Modoc and California Cattlemen's associations and has been a member of the Public Lands Council. Likely Land & Livestock has become a highly respected operation known for the quality of its beef.

A focal point to life at the ranch is the daily 6AM breakfast at the ranch cook-

BELOW: *Cowhands roping cattle. From* Great Ranches of the West, *pg. 67.*

RIGHT:
Contemporary cowhands

ABOVE:
Two horses framed by the weathered siding of a barn

LEFT:
Back lit dust silhouettes a frisky steer

house. Breakfast on many ranches traditionally can be the biggest meal of the day, but more importantly here it is also the one time the 3 brothers are together in their otherwise busy and separate work schedules. Around the breakfast table, in the company of a dedicated team of ranch hands, they plan and coordinate the day's chores and activities.

The Flournoy clan has prospered on the ranch for many generations, and one hopes that today their children and grandchildren will be inspired to continue the family business and confront the inevitable challenges the future will bring.

Sunrise at the ranch

FIVE DOT RANCH
STANDISH, CALIFORNIA
1959 [?]

One thing that is hard to find about the Five Dot Ranch land is information on its prior history. It is located in Lassen County near the town of Susanville, a former logging and mining town, established in 1857, which grew with the emigration of U.S. settlers following Mexico's cession of California and the Gold Rush of 1848. The area may have been too far north and remote from the coast to have enticed significant Spanish or Mexican settlement. With the east to west migration routes of U.S. citizens, however, it was a more reachable and logical destination.

Of note is that the owner of Five Dot Ranch, the Swickard family, goes back 7 generations to 1852, when Andrew Swickard and his wife Susannah first homesteaded in California's Santa Clara Valley and began ranching. Ultimately, their great grandson John August ("Jack") Swickard and his wife, Margaret, with the help of his parents, John and Evelyn Swickard, moved their operation to Standish, a small town east of Susanville, and, in 1959, started the Five Dot Land & Cattle Company with 200 head of cattle. Jack's brother Tom soon joined them.

The ranch headquarters they inherited had been developed much earlier, and included the Victorian style farmhouse, which was built in 1890 over a rock-walled root cellar constructed in 1880. The house was added on to in 1950, prior to the Swickards' purchase and has subsequently been remodeled and added to, most recently in 1999.

Over the years the ranch's cattle operation has focused primarily on Angus cattle. In 1994, Jack and Margaret's son Todd and his wife Loretta took over the daily management of the ranch and transitioned operations to an all-natural, mostly grass-fed program. By 2007, the family was fully committed to locally bred cattle ("from birth to plate") free of any antibiotics or hormones, and raised with what is known as "low stress" han-

A December frost

BELOW: *Getting ready for the roundup (top). John Harvey Swickard, 1917. Photo courtesy of Five Dot Ranch (bottom).*
RIGHT: *Roundup*

*The Victorian-era farmhouse behind old
Poplar trees*

dling, all engineered to improve the quality of beef product.

Above and beyond the cattle operation, the family is also working conscientiously with local, state and federal agencies and environmental groups such as the Natural Resources Conservation Service and California Fish and Wildlife to manage and restore the natural landscape and its many wild native species, and to assure that their grazing program is as harmonious as possible with the natural environment. Working commercial ranches are fewer and farther between, but Five Dot represents one of the finest and most successful examples of those that survive.

ABOVE AND LEFT:
Farmhouse interiors

The farmhouse kitchen

LEFT:
Weathered barns

FOLLOWING PAGES:
The main gate

FIVE DOT RA

PIEDRA BLANCA RANCHO

SAN SIMEON, CALIFORNIA

1865

Piedra Blanca Rancho is perhaps not as well known as its neighbor, San Simeon's much toured Hearst Castle, but the castle, ambitiously built by William Randolph Hearst with architect Julia Morgan and completed in 1947, would not have happened but for his father George Hearst's original purchase of the spectacular ranch property in 1865.

The history of the ranch began even earlier, in 1840, when 48,806 acres was granted by the new Mexican Governor Juan Alvarado to José de Jesús Pico from Monterey. George Hearst was among the early buyers and acquired a majority of the rancho in his first purchase in 1865. Hearst continued to acquire additional adjacent land when available. Following George Hearst's death in 1891, his widow Phoebe Apperson Hearst also expanded the family's ranch holdings until her death in 1919. Their son, William Randolph Hearst, bought an adjoining 153,000 acres, bringing the ranch to a total of over 250,000 acres by 1925.

For George Hearst, the ranch was perhaps of secondary interest to his pursuit of mining investments and later serving as a United States senator beginning in 1886, but he did spend time there on camping trips with the young William, who developed a more intense relationship with the ranch and a devotion to its magnificent scenery.

Following his first purchase, George built the wharf and warehouse on the bay and a number of the wood-clad barn and ranch buildings at Piedra Blanca, including the Victorian ranch house in 1878, which was comfortable enough that his wife and guests could visit more frequently. George had a side interest in raising thoroughbred racehorses, but following his death it was William who eventually took a more avid interest in expanding and developing the ranch into a working cattle ranch.

Through the years while he was building his powerful journalistic empire, he also built ambitiously as a rancher, en-

A fanciful wrought iron sign at the main gate

122 Piedra Blanca Rancho

Hearst Ranch Cowboys lining up horses for a parade in nearby
Cambria in the 1920s. Photo from Hearst Ranch: Family, Land and Legacy, *pg. 90-91.*

listing Julia Morgan in the design and
construction not only of the castle but
also in that of a number of Mission and
Spanish Revival style accessory structures
on the ranch. These included houses for
Hearst employees at San Simeon, a grand
house for the poultry ranch manager, the
Pico Creek Stables, and an even more
elaborate and grander cowboy dormitory
or *bunkhouse* as it came to be known, for
visiting guests as well as ranch hands, the
last constructed in 1936 by the contractor
George Loorz, who at Morgan's recom-
mendation took over most of the building
from Hearst's original construction superintendent Camille Rossi. Hearst also built
a large hunting lodge in Jolon called the
Hacienda, which was later acquired by the
U.S. Army in 1940 when Hearst sold them
the 154,000 acre Milpitas ranch, now the
Fort Hunter Liggett army base. None of
these projects, of course, rivaled the Castle
on the Enchanted Hill at which Hearst fa-
mously entertained world leaders as well
as Hollywood royalty.

In 1957, six years after Hearst's death in
1951, the family and the Hearst Corporation donated the castle to the state of California, and it is now one of the most
successful and popular tourist attractions
in the state's park system. Piedra Blanca

ABOVE:
Post Office, San Simeon Village

LEFT:
Original 1878 Italianate-style Victorian ranch house

ABOVE: *Barn (top) and ranch office (bottom)*
RIGHT: *The 1936 Monterey Revival style "bunkhouse,"*
designed by Julia Morgan

Rancho, however, continues under the Hearst Corporation's ownership as a working cattle ranch, and most if not all of the ranch buildings are still used today just as they have been for many decades. The grass-fed cattle operation remains one of the finest in the state if not nation, and Hearst Ranch Beef products (and also now its vineyard wines) are sold by top markets such as Whole Foods Market. In 2005 the Hearst Corporation partnered with The California Rangeland Trust, The American Land Conservancy and the State of California to create the largest land conservation easement in California's history, ensuring the preservation of the ranch and its magnificent scenery in perpetuity.

SMALLER RANCHES

TRESCH RANCH

PETALUMA, CALIFORNIA
1905

Joe Tresch's family emigrated from Switzerland to California in the 1870s, and in 1905 his great grandparents and his paternal grandmother, Olympia Nonella Tresch, then 8 years old, settled the current ranch near Petaluma. It stayed in the family over the years, and in 1988 Joe purchased 320 acres from his stepmother and leased an additional 1,189 acres. Today Joe, his wife, Kathy, and their 3 children—Joey, Lindsay and Lydia—run a heard of about 900 Holstein milk cows on over 2,500 acres, and they are the largest supplier of cow's milk to the Straus Family Creamery.

The ranch occupies a picturesque setting in an area called "Olympia's Valley" (after Joe's grandmother) in southwestern Sonoma County. It might well not have survived because in 1987 the County of Sonoma selected a portion of the property for a landfill dump. Narrowly escaping this first threat, a year later the Tresch family confronted another: the neighboring City of Santa Rosa attempted to acquire over half the land to create a sewage reservoir. The Tresch and Straus families, along with others, fought the proposed plan in a court battle and six years later finally prevailed.

In addition to these neighboring challenges from suburban expansion, the Tresches have kept pace in the dairy industry with the conversion to organic farming. In the 1970s, larger corporate dairy farms appeared to be taking over in the area, feeding larger herds with purchased feeds and using more chemically driven agricultural systems, and the consequently smaller family farms went into decline. More recently, however, the Straus Family Creamery, founded in 1994 by Albert Straus and dedicated to organic practices, has supported the growth of smaller organic family farms, including the Treschs's, which converted first a portion of their herd to organic and, ultimately, their entire ranch to a pasture-based and herbicide-free operation.

140

In addition to their collaboration with
the creamery, the ranch has developed
other sources of revenue as well, including an organic apple orchard, calf and
organic beef raising programs, and agricultural produce. They have also opened
the ranch to table dinners, weddings and
charity events, as well as the occasional
television and movie location shooting.
Today the ranch house interior is deco-
rated with an abundance of Americana
and western memorabilia. When the
artist Cristo conceived and realized his
work *Running Fence* between 1972 and
1976, the Tresch Ranch was one of a

contiguous string of properties participating in the art installation. Although
their main milk cow operation continues, the job of protecting and preserving
their land and lifestyle has engaged the
Tresch family in enterprises which a
generation or two ago they might never
have imagined.

ABOVE:
Western-themed memorabilia adorns the walls

OPPOSITE:
A detail of the fireplace

FOLLOWING PAGES:
The bar

ABOVE:
A peaceful spot by the pond

RIGHT:
Dairy cows resting in the pasture

MOORE RANCH

NICASIO, CALIFORNIA
1844/1922

The small town of Nicasio (population 96) in Marin County north of San Francisco might be best known today for George Lucas's Skywalker Ranch, a part of Lucasfilm Ltd., which lies within the township. Nicasio's history, however, owed its origin in the nineteenth century to timber, fishing and agricultural activities during the Mexican occupation.

The original 80,000-acre Rancho Nicasio was granted by Mexico's Governor José Figueroa in 1835 to the Coast Miwok tribe, but their claim was later rejected by the U.S. Public Land Commission in 1855. Apparently disregarding this earlier grant, Governor Manuel Micheltorena granted 56,621 acres of the rancho in 1844 to John B.R. Cooper, an Anglo sea captain, and Pablo de la Guerra, a Spanish nobleman, as payment for their part in the Mexican War of Independence. Subsequently, they granted 9,500 acres to their surveyor, Jasper O'Farrell, who in turn sold it to James Black. Black, a

Scottish sailor, had been stranded in California having contracted Typhus. He built the first building in Nicasio and established a cattle cooperative for local dairy and beef ranchers. Black's family continued to own the acreage, which includes the Moore Ranch, until 1922, when it was leased by Edward and Mary Gallagher. The original main ranch house, which dates to the nineteenth century and has Victorian-era detailing, is part of a compound which includes a large barn, horse barn, bunkhouse, creamery and greenhouse.

For many years the Gallagher family produced milk for the Point Reyes Creamery and the Nicasio Cheese Factory while at the same time raising beef and pork for San Francisco markets. The Gallaghers finally purchased the ranch in 1947, and their sons continued the cattle ranching operation. In 1999 they sold the now 1,000-acre ranch to its current owners, Jim and Margaret Moore.

Goats playing around the "rock pile"

The main ranch house

Jim Moore was raised in Colorado and was familiar with the impact the twentieth century could have on a vanishing rural landscape. Soon after purchasing the ranch, the Moores established an agricultural easement with the Marin Agricultural Land Trust (MALT) to limit the ranch's holdings to agricultural uses, prevent its subdivision, and ensure its preservation forever. MALT agreements currently protect over 45,000 acres and some 70 ranches in Marin County.

The Moores painstakingly refurbished the original buildings and made sure they kept the character and heritage of this historic property. Today the ranch has organic orchards and gardens, horses, a herd of goats and a sizeable pond that ducks and geese call home. Wild turkeys, owls, falcons and hawks are regular visitors. The family has planted several hundred native oak and cypress trees and restored over two miles of riparian habitat. There are still deer and cows grazing, and when visitors come up the half mile driveway they are taken

Kitchen

back to the 1800s and the "California" rural lifestyle that once existed throughout the state.

The ranch has provided commercial location shots to companies like William Sonoma, Orvis, L.L. Bean, Coldwater Creek and Lands End. These companies might like their customers to believe a rural lifestyle is still a common California phenomenon, but only a few ranches like the Moore's offer up such suitable scenery. Although the MALT agricultural easement should endure, the rustic setting may soon change, as the Moores have recently put their ranch up for sale. The land will survive, but what may happen to the buildings under new ownership is another question.

LEFT: *Canada geese on the pond*

ABOVE: *The nineteenth-century horse barn (top); favorite horses, Boris and Spike (bottom)*

FOLLOWING PAGES: *Horse barn*

CAÑADA LARGA RANCH

VENTURA, CALIFORNIA
1841

The original Rancho Cañada Larga o Verde was a 6,659-acre Mexican land grant by Governor Juan B. Alvarado made to Joquina Alvarado in 1841. Joquina was the widow of Gabriel Anotonio Moraga, a notable member of the Spanish military. Following the cession of California to the U.S., Joquina's claim was patented in 1873. A year later in 1874, a Frenchman, Anselme Canet, and his family moved from New York City to Ventura where he entered the cattle business and acquired Rancho Cañada Larga o Verde. Over the years separate parcels of the property were sold and operated as smaller ranching and farming concerns, including walnut and apricot groves.

In the early 1970s George Randolph Hearst Jr., grandson of William Randolph Hearst (see p. 120), acquired 1,500 acres of the original Canet holdings from various owners in an attempt to reassemble the original ranch. Hearst lived on the ranch for over 20 years, raising his children and running cattle. He built an equestrian facility with the idea initially of staging rodeos but eventually became more interested in breeding and raising cutting horses.

In 1989, Steve Gaggero purchased 1,980 acres adjacent to Hearst's ranch from Bertha Thoming, who was at the time in her 90s. Bertha was the granddaughter of Gabriel Bordenave, who had acquired the original land grant. In 1996, Gaggero was able to purchase the Hearst ranch as well and combine it with his Bordenave holdings, creating the current Cañada Larga Ranch and comprising nearly 3,500 acres.

Today the ranch accommodates a modest grass-fed beef operation, along with an equestrian facility of approximately 100-120 horses, and a 3,000-tree olive orchard and organic olive oil business.

Ranch headquarters with leftover trees from the former walnut and apricot orchards in the foreground

ABOVE:
*George Hearst double-wide
trailer ranch house, ca. 1970s.
Photo courtesy of Steve Gaggero.*

RIGHT:
*One of the original ranch houses,
now the ranch offices*

FOLLOWING PAGES:
*The double-wide trailer ranch house today,
embellished with "log cabin" siding*

A bedroom

ABOVE:
The equestrian center's large riding arena

FOLLOWING PAGES:
The ranch house and tree house among a grouping of Sycamore trees

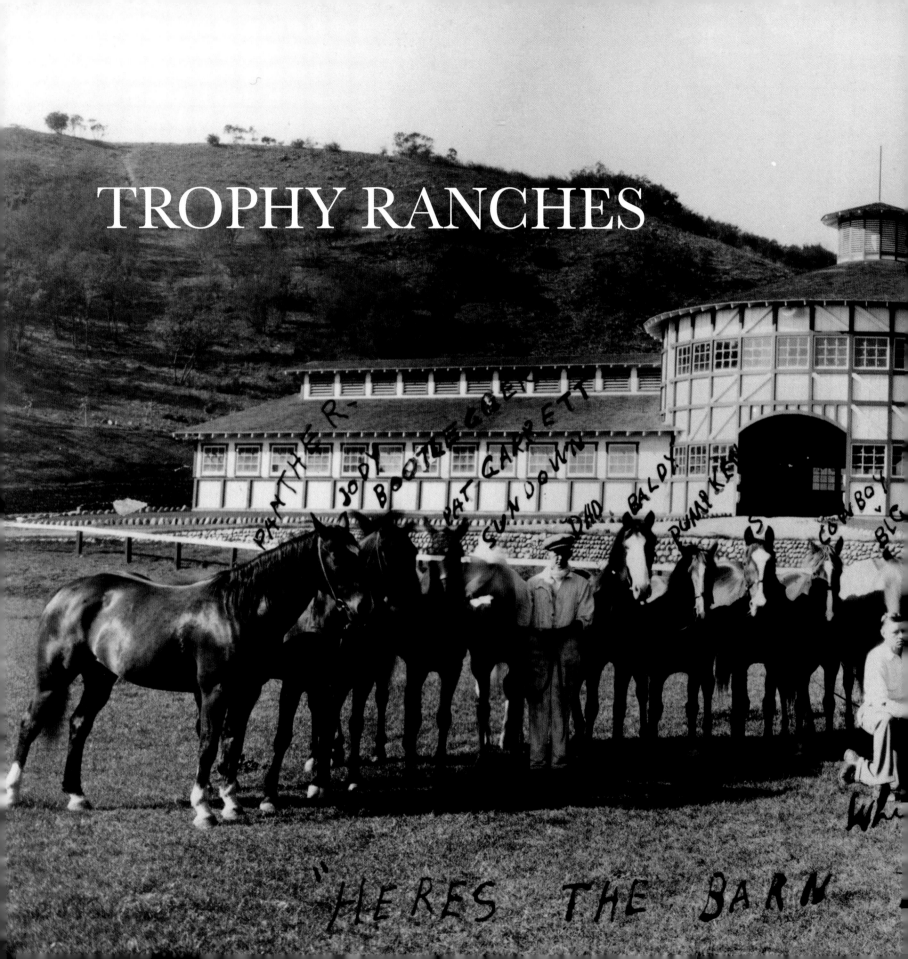

TROPHY RANCHES

WILL ROGERS RANCH

PACIFIC PALISADES, CALIFORNIA
1925

Surely one of the smallest ranches at 186 acres (and also one where the only calf was a stuffed one in his living room that Will Rogers used for roping practice), this ranch still captivates today as a realization of idealized western ranch culture. The ranch land was once part of the much larger Rancho Boca de Santa Monica, granted in 1838 by the Mexican Republic to Francisco Marquez and Ysidro Reyes. By the end of the nineteenth century, most of the original rancho had been divided and sold, and in the early twentieth century, Robert Conran Gillis began acquiring tracts of the land to develop residential subdivisions. Among the neighborhoods he developed were Westgate, Brentwood, parts of Santa Monica and the Palisades, now among the wealthiest in western Los Angeles. In 1925, by which time these subdivisions were well underway, Will Rogers was fortunate enough to purchase a relatively untouched larger parcel.

Rogers was born in 1879 on a big ranch in Oologah on the Cherokee Nation near Claremont, now part of Oklahoma. In 1898 he became a cowboy in Texas on W.P. Ewing's Little Robe Ranch. His abilities as a trick roper landed him a job with Texas Jack's Wild West Circus in South Africa from 1902–1903. Over the years, Rogers added an engagingly homespun and humorous dialogue to his roping act, and he eventually joined the Ziegfeld Follies in 1916. He was well on his way to fame and fortune and becoming a major movie star, radio personality, columnist, and social and political satirist.

By 1920 he was an international celebrity, and he and his wife, Betty, were living in Beverly Hills and eager to find a weekend retreat, close to the city with easy access to his entertainment and business dealings but removed enough for him to get away from it all and reconnect with his cowboy roots. He found it with his 1925 purchase, a stone's throw from what was then Beverly Boulevard but which would become Sunset Boulevard, yet

secluded enough to feel like it was in the country.

He initially built a simple one-story cabin on the property, which would later be used for guests and servants, but in 1927 he began building his ranch house, a great high-ceiling room with an extended porch fronting a large lawn with panoramic ocean and mountain views. The room interior with its timber beams, wood board walls, stone fireplace and furnishings—including a wagon wheel—seemed inspired by a Hollywood western movie set, and it perfectly captured a rustic western lifestyle no doubt close to Rogers heart.

OPPOSITE:
*The ranch buildings nestled
behind California Live oak
and Pepper trees*

RIGHT:
*Roger's eventual ranch house
from 1927, with some of the
taxidermy he used for roping
practice*

The dining room with portraits of
Betty and Will Rogers

Soon after completing the ranch house,
he commissioned architect Frederick Ken
Reese to add a large two-story Monterey
Colonial style bedroom wing to the
north. Ernest A. Batchelder—the famous
tile-maker from Pasadena—was brought
in to fit out fireplaces and bathrooms. By
1930, Will and Betty had moved perma-
nently to the ranch from Beverly Hills.

The ranch complex, including the 1926
polo field, had quickly expanded to include paddocks, a riding arena and a
number of outbuildings. By far the
largest of these structures and the centerpiece of the compound was an impressive twenty-stall horse barn with a central
training ring topped by a cupola on the
roof. The barn was Rogers's pride and
joy. A life-long horseman, he was fond of
claiming that he had a nicer barn for his
horses than he did a house for his family.

During their years at the ranch, the
Rogers family welcomed many famous
people from the entertainment industry.
Guests included the likes of Walt Disney,

Douglas Fairbanks Jr., Darryl Zanuck, Hal Roach, Clark Gable and Gary Cooper, many of whom came to play polo. Rogers had become a much-loved and sought after celebrity, appreciated for his humor and perceptive wit. A great advocate for the aviation industry, Rogers met an untimely death in 1935 in a plane crash with the pilot Wiley Post. Although he was only 55 years old, our nation probably never had a better or wiser ambassador.

Betty and the children continued to live on the ranch until her death in 1944. She had already bequeathed the ranch to the state. It became a California State Park, open to the public, with its eques-

ABOVE: *A stable resident (top);
the barn's lofty central training ring space (bottom)*

RIGHT: *Barn exterior, with central
circular training ring to the right*

*The south-facing ranch house
and porch*

trian facilities for a long time available to
neighboring horse owners. In 1971 the
ranch house was listed in the National
Register of Historic Places, and Will
Rogers State Historic Park is today supported by the Will Rogers Ranch Foundation. The ranch house interior is
considered one of the most iconic examples of romanticized western décor,
something Rogers himself would no
doubt have dismissed with a clever aside.

BEAUTY RANCH

GLEN ELLEN, CALIFORNIA
1905

The charming town of Glen Ellen (population approximately 1,000) lies in Sonoma County north of San Francisco in an area indigenous tribes called "The Valley of the Moon." The town began when in 1859 Charles V. Stuart purchased part of an 1840 Rancho Agua Caliente Mexican land grant to Lazano Piña. He planted a vineyard named after his wife, Ellen, and soon the town grew up around it.

The famous writer Jack London was born in San Francisco in 1876, and spent much of his early years on adventurous travels to Japan, London and the Yukon, travels that were to inspire his writing. When he first visited Glen Ellen in 1903, married and already the father of two children, London fell passionately in love with Charmian Kittredge, and also seems to have been taken with the countryside around Glen Ellen. By 1905 he had divorced his first wife, married Charmian and purchased the first of several adjoining properties he was soon to acquire and call the Beauty Ranch. Farming and ranching in the area had not proved to be the promised land the early settlers had hoped for, and London, riding on his success as a writer, was able to easily acquire several failed properties. At the time he wrote:

At the present moment I am the owner of six bankrupt ranches, united in my possession. The six bankrupt ranches represent at least eighteen bankruptcies; that is to say, at least eighteen farmers of the old school have lost their money, broken their hearts, lost their land. The challenge to me is this: by using my head, my judgement, and all the latest knowledge in the matter of farming, can I make a success where these eighteen men have failed? I have pledged myself, my manhood, my future, my books and all that I possess to this undertaking.

ABOVE:
Charmian's sleeping porch, where Jack London died

OPPOSITE:
The clapboard cottage, originally part of the Kohler and Frohling Winery, which became the Londons' house

FOLLOWING PAGES:
London's study, desks and typewriter

London's assistant's desk. A photo of London's favorite horse, a shire stallion, is pictured in the photo above the lamp.

With this, London began idealistically on the eleven-year agricultural adventure that was to consume the rest of his short life. Inspired not only by a tenacious personality but by agricultural techniques and methods he had gleaned both academically as well as from his travels, he began various experimental ranching and farming projects, including growing spineless cactus for cattle feed, eucalyptus groves for timber, an elaborately designed piggery ("The Pig Palace") for raising hogs, and various other livestock and farming experiments. Many of these were to meet with mixed results.

Jack and Charmian traveled frequently, including a planned around-the-world voyage on their yacht *The Snark*, on which they reached the Hawaiian Islands, the Marquesas, Tahiti, Samoa, Fiji and other South Seas destinations, where he became quite sick. All the while, he continued an ambitious building program back home at Beauty Ranch. One of his purchases was the former Kohler and Frohling Winery, which included a

number of barn buildings as well as a clapboard cottage, which became Jack's and Charmian's residence while planning and building their dream house, a grand structure called Wolf House designed by San Francisco architect Albert Farr. Unfortunately Wolf House burned down in 1913 as it was nearing completion, and although London vowed to re-build it, this was never to be. The ruins of its impressive stone foundation, walls and chimneys remain today, the ghost of a dream.

London and Charmian persevered, but his health was in decline, and he died on November 22, 1916, as he lay on his bed on the sleeping porch of the cot-

ABOVE:
The smaller building to the left was the Manure Pit.

OPPOSITE:
The stone cottage dining room. The piano was a gift from London to his wife, Charmian.

BELOW:
The "Pig Palace," London's experiment in raising hogs

RIGHT:
*The stone wall ruins of the wine barrel rooms of the Kohler
and Frohling Winery, with vineyards beyond*

tage. He was 40 years old. After London's
death, Charmian inherited the ranch,
and she and Jack's stepsister Eliza Shepard and her family continued on there,
managing his creation as best they could
and hosting visiting family and friends.
Eliza died in 1939, Charmian in 1955.
The Shepard family retained some land,
but in 1959 a portion of the property was
donated to the state, establishing Jack
London State Historic Park. The Park
would eventually include 1,400 acres,
comparable to the original Beauty
Ranch, but it struggled to survive. Since

1984, the Valley of the Moon Natural History Association (now Jack London Park Partners) assisted the state's Department of Parks and Recreation with exhibits and fundraising. In 2012 this non-profit began operating the park, transitioning it to a successful enterprise with increased visitation and a rich program of public and private events—Jack London's visionary spirit still very much a palpable presence.

JOEL MCCREA RANCH

THOUSAND OAKS, CALIFORNIA
1934

The actors Joel McCrea and Will Rogers were close friends, and in the early 1930s Rogers, who had already purchased his ranch, advised McCrea to do the same and have something to fall back on if his acting career didn't work out. Needless to say, McCrea went on to have a long and successful career in movies through the 1970s, but he took his friend's advice anyway.

The McCrea Ranch is located in the Santa Rosa Valley at the base of the Norwegian Grade in Ventura County. The land had been previously used for cattle ranching and agricultural fields, and was part of the original 113,000 acre Rancho Simi, granted to the Pico brothers in 1795 and later patented to the de la Guerra family in 1865. The property was subsequently sold several times and subdivided, and in 1890 a portion was purchased by August DuMortier. When DuMortier died in 1895, the property was sold again and passed through several hands before being acquired by McCrea in 1933.

McCrea was not just an acting cowboy with a trophy ranch, but ran a 2,400-acre working cattle ranch he, his wife, the actress Frances Dee, and their children called home. McCrea and his wife raised three sons—Jody, David and Peter—on the ranch and were active in the local community.

Immediately after buying the property, Joel McCrea hired architect John Byers to design a new main ranch house. In 1928 Byers had designed a house for McCrea's mother, but he was also a natural choice given his stylistic penchant for modest vernacular California ranch architecture. The board and batten house is still standing today, furnished much as it was when occupied by the McCreas.

In the late 1950s and early '60s, parts of the ranch were sold for housing, and today only some 280 acres of the original ranch remain. Joel McCrea died in 1990, and in 1995 the family donated the remainder of the ranch to the Conejo Recreation and Park District.

Main ranch house designed for the McCreas by architect John Byers in 1934

All of the ranch buildings, including the main house, were placed on the National Register of Historic Places in 1997. Frances McCrea continued to live there until her death in 2004.

The Park District has begun to schedule programs for public access and a 1,400-square-foot visitor center has recently been built. The Joel and Frances McCrea Ranch Foundation, which is supported by the McCrea family, assists in raising and managing funds to foster the Park Districts programs, share the McCrea family's history and preserve and restore the ranch buildings. Wyatt McCrea, whose father, David, grew up on the ranch, knew his grandfather well. He has a direct and personal connection to the family's legacy, has lived on the ranch for nearly 30 years, and he and his wife Lisa are the principal force behind the family foundation.

ABOVE:
The master bedroom

OPPOSITE:
A George Washington seal adorns the living room fireplace

The present ranch office and visitor's center. A yellow "Banksiae" rose vine entwines the fence

*Lisa McCrea riding
through a field of
flowering mustard*

ABOVE: *The old milk house (top)*
and milk house paraphernalia within (bottom)

RIGHT: *Remnants of a freight wagon from the old days*

FOLLOWING PAGES:
Eucalyptus trees line the road to the main house

FRENCH RANCH

THOUSAND OAKS, CALIFORNIA
1926

Major Leigh Hill French was born in 1863 in Dover, New Hampshire, worked as a cowboy and stagecoach driver in Texas as a young man, and inherited the Howe's London Circus, touring the country with the show. He earned degrees in law, medicine and engineering, and became a gentleman adventurer and entrepreneur. He rode with Teddy Roosevelt and the Rough Riders in Cuba in 1898, served in the First World War, and pioneered the early development of the Alaska Territory, where he helped build the first railroad. While sojourning in Alaska, he also apparently met Jack London (see p. 192). During his lifetime, French made and lost several fortunes speculating in oil and mining.

At the age of 57, he met, seduced and won the hand of his young twenty-one year old bride-to-be, Eleanor Brown, a student at Wellesley College, while she was visiting her brother in California. In 1926 the couple purchased (with *her* family's money!) approximately 4,000 acres of ranch land in the Protrero Valley near Las Turas Lake in what was later to become known as Hidden Valley.

The Frenches subdivided the ranch and in 1929 commissioned the Santa Monica architect John Winford Byers to design and build an ambitious Spanish Colonial Revival style ranch house with a second story Monterey Colonial balcony. Byers, a self-trained architect, got his start as a builder who initially manufactured many of his own materials. The main house and its compound of accessory structures, which include a windmill/pump house, bunk house, stables and feed barn, offer a remote picturesque setting situated in a valley at the end of a country road, surrounded by over 100,000 acres of county, state and federal lands. They eventually moved into the house when they received an offer on an adjacent ranch house in which they had been living.

Major French died in 1941, and his ashes are buried alongside his mother's, be-

A newly purchased prize admired by local horsemen at the French Ranch, ca. 1925. From Ranches of the American West, *pg. 281.*

neath a massive oak tree in the garden behind the house he and his wife had originally conceived as a "spec" house and
"trophy" ranch property. Mrs. French,
who was to survive her husband by some
50 years, continued to live in the house.
She ran Whiteface Hereford cattle on the
ranch, was an obsessive dog-lover and became well known over the years as quite a
colorful local character before she died at
the age of 92.

From time to time starting in the 1930s,
the ranch was used for movie and television location shoots. Among the movies

PREVIOUS PAGES: *The main house, originally designed by John Byers in 1929, burned in 1982 but has been rebuilt.*

ABOVE: *Front porch with cactus garden (top); main gallery (bottom)*

RIGHT: *The living room, with tiled stair to loft aboveion*

shot there were the *Tom Mix film Destry Rides Again* (1932), four Roy Rogers and Gene Autry films, Warner Brothers' *The Lone Ranger* (1956) and the pilot for the television series *Bonanza*.

In 1982, the original house was largely destroyed by an electrical fire. Its new owner, Joel Shukovsky, whose own career as a movie and TV producer had a coincidental connection to the ranch's history, saw an opportunity when he purchased it from the French family estate. Shukovsky spent the next several years working with 3 different architects, meticulously rebuilding the house on the existing foundation and referencing Byers's original plans. A New Yorker but a passionate student of the Spanish Colonial Revival style with an eye for detail, Shukovsky has added his own eclectic touches

PAGES 232–233:
The kitchen with its exuberant tile work (at left); cockfight light fixtures (at right)

OPPOSITE:
Library and bar (left of fireplace)

RIGHT:
A bedroom

ABOVE:
Dovecote and stables

OPPOSITE:
Brangus cattle

Major French's ashes, as well as his mother's, are buried beneath the large oak seen through the archway.

and furnishings and now calls it "Land Grant Revival Style." Although more ambitious still than Byers' accomplishment, the end result nevertheless retains the romantic spirit of the original. Today, Shukovsky lives in the house and raises a small herd of Brangus cattle on what is now approximately 200 acres.

RANCHES IN
TRANSITION

HOLLISTER RANCH

GAVIOTA, CALIFORNIA
1822/1834

The land comprising Hollister Ranch is spectacularly picturesque, bordering the Pacific coast between Point Conception to the west and Gaviota State Park to the east. Originally occupied by the Native American Chumash Indians, it was probably first seen by Spanish explorers in 1769, when Don Gaspar de Portola and Padre Juan Crespi travelled through the Santa Barbara region. José Francisco de Ortega, one of the Portola expedition scouts, founded the presidio in Santa Barbara in 1782, and on his retirement in 1991 he was granted a grazing permit for Rancho Nuestra Señora del Refugio, which included the Hollister Ranch. Ortega died in 1798, and it was only much later in 1822 that his family was granted legal title from Spain.

With the Mexican War of Independence from Spain and the formation of the new government, the Ortega family was forced in 1829 to petition again for title, which for a second time was eventually granted in 1834. Although the family managed to hold on to the rancho follow-ing the U.S. occupation and conquest of California in 1848, by 1866 portions of land had been sold to the Dibblee/Hollister partnerships. That partnership dissolved in 1881, with William W. Hollister taking control of, among other ranchos, Rancho Nuestra Señora del Refugio.

Hollister, who was born in 1818 and grew up in Ohio, became a successful sheep farmer, immigrated to California, and in his later years settled in the Santa Barbara area. Although he never held office, he was a generous contributor to the community and died there in 1886. Hollister never lived on the Hollister Ranch property, but one of his sons, John James Hollister, became superintendent of the ranch in 1899, and he and his wife Lottie relocated there, eventually moving into what was called the "Big House" in Bulito Canyon in 1910.

Three things happened, one during this period and two much later, that were to make a lasting and not altogether positive impact on the ranch: in 1899 the South-

ern Pacific Railroad negotiated a 60 foot
wide easement across Hollister Ranch
which followed the coastline. Although the
railroad had agreed to construct trestles
across the many canyons so as to keep the
views and coastal access open, they failed
to do so at Santa Anita Canyon, the original site of the Hollister family home. A
much later encroachment happened in
1961 when major oil companies constructed pipelines through the ranch.
About that time as well, the scenic coastline of the ranch was discovered by surfers
to be one of the prime surfing spots in
California.

The Hollister Estate Company was incorporated in 1910, and James continued to
manage the ranch until his death in 1961,
five years after his wife Lottie had died.
Their children agreed to sell the ranch and
in 1964 it was optioned by a group of
twelve attorney-developers. The buyers
were unsuccessful in their development
plans, as was a subsequent buyer, Macco
Realty, but a third developer, the Mortgage
Guarantee Insurance Corporation took

title in 1970 and was ultimately successful in subdividing the 14,400 acre ranch into 135 parcels and instituting a Homeowner's Association, common lands permitting only agricultural use, and conditions prohibiting further subdivisions. It was no accident that a number of the first buyers were avid surfers. The Hollister Ranch Homeowners' Association took over control in 1976. The association manages the property today with the assistance of the Hollister Ranch Cattle Cooperative as well as the Hollister Ranch Conservancy, which was established to protect the natural environment of the ranch. The cooperative, which includes most of the homeowners, grazes cattle according to an arrangement and in cooperation with the conservancy, which has not always been easy but which the majority of the homeowners support.

John McCarty, who has been ranch manager for the cattle cooperative for over four decades, has been instrumental in all this, maintaining a working grass-fed cattle operation while juggling the concerns of the homeowner's association and the conser-

vancy. Several of the homeowners have been actively involved with the cattle operation as well, volunteering a significant amount of their time and effort towards what appears to be an unusual and, so far it seems, successful partnership between ranching and development.

LEFT:
*Sue Benech Field, resident
and regular ranch volunteer*

FOLLOWING PAGES:
*One of the Hollister
homeowner's properties*

PAICINES RANCH
PAICINES, CALIFORNIA
1842

Pulling off route 156 onto route 25 south of Hollister and heading through Tres Pinos towards San Benito, one passes relatively new suburban developments with green golf courses, the San Benito County Fairgrounds, a few vineyards, but then also some very dry ranchlands, drier than usual perhaps on account of today's drought conditions. It is refreshing to finally turn into the entrance to Paicines Ranch. One feels there, as well, the impact of the drought but is also aware of the ranch's more lush cienegas adjacent to the San Benito River.

Rancho Cienega de los Paicines has been a working cattle ranch since it was first granted to Angel Castro and Jose Rodriguez in 1842, who in turn sold it to Francisco Villegas. By 1867 it belonged to Alexander Grogan, an Irish settler who had been successful in real estate and commodities speculation in San Francisco.

Grogan ran a dairy operation on the ranch and by the 1880s had built many of the oldest buildings, including the Grogan House and two large barns. He died in 1886, and the ranch passed to his sister and two other owners, but in 1906 it was purchased by George Sykes and Kinglsey Macomber. The ranch was subdivided and Macomber took the part which comprises today's Paicines Ranch and included the principal buildings. It was Macomber who had a penchant for Spanish-Moorish architecture and subsequently added stables, a circular water tank, garage and new residence inspired by this somewhat eclectic aesthetic.

In 1927, Macomber sold the ranch to Walter Murphy from Chicago, a friend of President Franklin Roosevelt. The president's wife Eleanor visited the ranch, and their son, Jimmy, apparently spent a year there recuperating from an illness. In 1943 the ranch was again sold, this time to Robert and Katherine Law. During their tenure, Sid Luft and Judy Garland were married in the Grogan House, and the Laws also developed extensive vineyards during the 1960s. In

A deciduous valley oak in its winter state, with barn beyond

ABOVE:
*Front porch wind break
at Grogan House*

RIGHT:
*A view of the guest
cottage framed by trees*

ABOVE:
Spanish-Moorish style circular water tank

1989 it was bought by the Ridgemark Corporation, which had designs to develop the ranch into a resort hotel and golf course with residential housing.

Perhaps needless to say, the corporation's grand plans never materialized, and in 2001 the ranch was purchased by its current owners, Sallie Calhoun and her husband Matt Christiano, both successful Silicon Valley entrepreneurs, as their weekend retreat. They have also tried to maintain cattle and agricultural operations while at the same time expanding their marketing to include weddings, corporate events, conferences, reunions and training classes, as well as horse boarding.

*Grogan House, built by
Alexander Grogan in
the 1880s*

Grogan House
interiors

ABOVE:
*Macomber-era Spanish-
Moorish stables can be
glimpsed in the distance
beyond California
pepper trees.*

RIGHT:
Guest cottage

ABOVE: *Barn built by Alexander Grogan, ca. 1867. From East of the Gabilans, p. 140, (top). Barn, ca. 1880s (bottom).*

LEFT: *Silos, mill and barns*

RANCHO SAN CARLOS

CARMEL VALLEY, CALIFORNIA
1835

Rancho San Carlos was on land once occupied by a Native American tribe called the Costanoan Rumsen Ohlone. The founding of the Mission San Carlos Borroméo de Carmelo and the Presidio in Monterey in 1770 established the area as an important religious and military center during both the Spanish and Mexican occupations, but initiated the decline of the indigenous culture.

Following the secularization of the missions in 1834, two land grants were given by Governor Juan Alvarado: the first, San Francisquito, in 1835 to Estévan Munrás and his wife Catalina Manzanelli Munrás, and the second, El Portrero de San Carlos, in 1837 to a Mission Indian whose Christian name was Fructuoso del Real. Rancho San Carlos included portions of both these ranchos, which changed hands several times until finally being acquired by four brothers named Sargent, who had also amassed numerous other holdings in San Joaquin, Santa Clara and Monterey counties. The brothers later divided up their real estate empire, and the San Francisquito and Potrero de San Carlos portions both went to Bradley Sargent in 1876. Bradley and his wife, Julie Flynn, named their ranch San Francisquito y San Carlos. Sargent and later his son, Bradley Jr., were involved through the end of the nineteenth century in politics in Monterey County and the state.

The Scottish author Robert Louis Stevenson (*Treasure Island, Kidnapped*) had a passionate love affair with an American married woman named Fanny Osbourne while traveling in France in 1879; he followed her back to California, only to discover that she was unwilling to divorce her philandering husband. Lovesick and suffering from a severe lung infection while in Monterey, he ventured on horseback up the Carmel Valley and passed out on a portion of Bradley Sargent's ranch, to be rescued by a family who had been farming a small tract within the ranch. The family nursed him back to health, and the previously reluctant Fanny—apparently swayed by

The original Casa Grande built by George Moore in 1926 and now called "The Hacienda."

272

BELOW: *The Hacienda fireplace alcove*
RIGHT: *The main living room of the Hacienda*

FOLLOWING PAGES: *Mature native Madrone trees (*Arbutus menziesii*) shade the Hacienda's outdoor dining courtyard.*

Stevenson's plight—finally agreed to divorce her husband and subsequently married Stevenson.

In 1923, the 23,000-acre ranch entered a momentous chapter in its history: George Gordon Moore, an adventurous New York entrepreneur (and speculated by some to be the model for F. Scott Fitzgerald's novel *The Great Gatsby*) purchased the ranch from the Sargent heirs and renamed it Rancho San Carlos. The flamboyant Moore loved hunting, polo and entertaining lavishly. Among other indulgences, Moore introduced a dozen wild boars from his North Carolina hunting

preserve onto the ranch, and it is presumably from this initial population—interbred with feral and domestic pigs—that wild boars have now spread throughout much of central California and are still a presence (and occasional nuisance) on the ranch to this day.

Soon after buying the property, Moore began an ambitious building program to create a "gentleman's" ranch. In 1926, he employed the Carmel contractor M.J. Murphy to design and build a large home which he called Casa Grande, and also constructed stables, a stud barn, polo field, dam and lake. The house—loosely inspired by Spanish/Mexican hacienda precedents in a pueblo revival style—was a grand af-

LEFT AND ABOVE:
Guest house wing of the Hacienda (left) and porch (above)

fair including many guest rooms and living areas catering to Moore's penchant for entertaining industry moguls and Hollywood royalty. It is a testament to Moore's ambitious building program that the house was later able to easily accommodate its function today as a gracious members-only inn and restaurant.

With the Depression, Moore held on to the ranch with difficulty and in 1939 finally lost it to creditors, who sold it to Arthur C. Oppenheimer, a wealthy San Francisco businessman, who persuaded

one of his favorite stewards at the Alameda Yacht Club, George King, to manage the estate as both a family retreat and working cattle ranch. For almost 50 years, the ranch was well known for producing quality beef. Arthur Oppenheimer died in the late 1940s, and the ranch passed to his son, Arthur Jr. In the 1980s, the family leased grazing rights to neighboring ranchers and in 1990 sold it to the Rancho San Carlos Partnership, a group which developed plans for a unique private residential subdivision and wildlife preserve.

Although it took the partnership a number of years to achieve their goal, Rancho San Carlos—now also known as the

LEFT: *Horses at the equestrian center*
BELOW: *Old storage sheds*

20,000-acre Santa Lucia Preserve—has become a private community subdivision of almost 300 home sites, carefully planned so that the houses do not visually intrude on the natural scenery of the original ranch, 18,000 acres of which remain wilderness. Although a number of community amenities such as a golf course, clubhouse and equestrian and sports centers were added, a visit to the ranch is not that different than it was in George Moore's day, with many of the original buildings preserved. The original house or *hacienda* has been converted to an inn for members and guests with a restaurant and meeting rooms but its exterior is little

ABOVE: *The Ranch Center, ca. 1930.*
Photo courtesy of Santa Lucia Preserve.
RIGHT: *A view of the Hacienda*

changed and still the centerpiece of the
ranch. It helps that the ranch is remote
from civilization and a half-hour drive into
the mountains south of Carmel Valley, but
there are also strict home design guide-
lines, no individual property fences are al-
lowed, wildlife is free to roam, and a
nature conservation ethic is enforced by a
local conservancy group. In a limited, controlled program, cattle grazing has been
recently reintroduced and despite the evo-
lution and transformation of the property,
the development has succeeded in retain-
ing the appearance and much of the wild
environment of the original ranch.

BELCAMPO FARMS

MOUNT SHASTA, CALIFORNIA
2009

Belcampo Farms is by no means a historical California ranch and is a relatively new enterprise, but it might just represent a future alternative to conventional cattle ranching. We first read about Belcampo in a small article in *Sunset Magazine* from 2012, then again in a *New Yorker* profile on Anya Fernald, its co-founder and CEO. Although not fitting the typical ranch profile, the company's farm deserves notice alongside its more historic companions.

The 20,000-acre Belcampo Farms began not as an ancestral homestead, but as an idea—a business plan to provide healthy organic meat from field to table in a controlled yet economically viable way. Anya Fernald and Todd Robinson, the principal investor behind Belcampo, came into ranching backwards—from the restaurant and butcher shop. At stake is a philosophy and approach, inspired by Temple Grandin, to raising and processing animals more humanely. A big part of this is that Belcampo is not just a part of the process,

but the entire process, with control over its own livestock breeding, raising and feed, its own low-stress slaughterhouse (Belcampo Butchery), and even its own butcher shops and restaurants (Belcampo Meat Co.). It is banking that this will create a more desirable luxury product than the conventional industrialized meat process. With an ambitious marketing plan that includes recipes, it also preaches that our diet should include more of the whole rather than just select cuts of the animal, and not just beef, but other meats as well.

At the ranch near Mt. Shasta, not only cattle but sheep, goats, pigs, geese and chickens are being raised in a grass-fed open range setting. This could be sustainable farming on a religious mission, with the compound of bright contemporary barn buildings its avant-garde architectural cathedral. Allan Savory, the biologist and writer who helped pioneer holistic resource management grazing, was one of Fernald's early inspirations, and she and Belcampo Farms have con-

Belcampo's modern buildings, designed by architect Hans Baldauf, echo a new era in farm-to-table ranching.

LEFT: *The Belcampo kitchen/dining room*

BELOW: *View of the ranch land with Mt. Shasta in the distance*

FOLLOWING PAGES:
The dining room, displaying the day's menu

tinued to experiment with their processes and marketing strategies.

What the average big city dweller may likely have noticed are Belcampo's retail outlets, Belcampo Meat Co., which are designed after a formula combining restaurant and butcher shop. Time will tell how well Belcampo's enterprise will fare, but it represents a refreshing new perspective on ranching. Ironically, it harkens back to a day before "progress"

ABOVE: *The office conference room, Mt. Shasta reflected in window (top); Mt. Shasta in the distance (bottom)*

RIGHT: *The commercial kitchen*

and industrialized farming and ranching took over, back to a time that preceded long-range refrigerated transport, when there was less waste and the trip from farm to table was much shorter. Perhaps its new brand marketing is partly a cry for a return to the best of the past.

ABOVE: *Original barn, Belcampo Farms*

RIGHT: *Herding cattle*

FOLLOWING PAGES: *Mt. Shasta rises majestically over fields near Belcampo.*

A SELECTED BIBLIOGRAPHY

Andree, Herb. John Byers, *Domestic Architect in Southern California: 1919–ca. 1960.* MA Thesis, University of California, Santa Barbara, 1971.

Anschutz, Philip F. *Out Where the West Begins.* Denver, Colorado: Cloud Camp Press, LLC, 2015.

Artabras. *Ranching Traditions: A Group of Essays.* Artabras, a division of Abbeville Publishing Group, 1989.

Athearn, Robert G. *The Mythic West in Twentieth-Century America.* Lawrence, Kansas: University Press of Kansas, 1986.

Bancroft, Hubert H. *History of California*, vols 1-7. San Francisco, California: History Co., 1886–1890.

Barber, Dan. *The Third Plate: Field Notes on the Future of Food.* London, UK: Penguin Books, 2014.

Bauer, Helen. *California Rancho Days.* Sacramento, California: California State Department of Education, 1957.

Beach, John. "The Bay Area Tradition, 1890–1915." In *Bay Area Houses*, ed. Sally B. Woodbridge. New York, New York: Oxford University Press, 1976.

Beach, John. "Julia Morgan: An Architect from Oakland." In *Architectural Drawings* by Julia Morgan, exhibition catalog. Oakland, California: Oakland Museum, 1976.

Bean, Walton, James J. Rawls. *California: An Interpretive History.* New York, New York: McGraw-Hill, 1983.

Bell, Horace. *Reminiscences of a Ranger; or Early Times in Southern California.* Los Angeles, California, 1851; Santa Barbara, California, 1929. Bidwell, John. *Life in California Before the Gold Discovery.* Palo Alto, California: Lewis Osborne, 1969.

Bixby-Smith, Sarah. *Adobe Days.* Cedar Rapids, Iowa, 1925. Boutelle, Sara Holmes. *Julia Morgan Architect: Revised and Updated Edition.* New York, New York: Abbeville Press, 1995.

Boutelle, Sara Holmes. "Julia Morgan." In *Women in Architecture: a Historic and Contemporary Perspective*, ed. Susana Torre. New York, New York: Whitney Library Design, 1977.

Brands, H.W. *The Age of Gold: The California Gold Rush and the American Dream.* New York, New York: Anchor Books, 2002.

Browne, T.M. *The Musgrove Ranch: A Tale of Southern California.* London, United Kingdom: Forgotten Books, 2012.

Carrillo, Leo. *The California I Love.* Englewood Cliffs, New Jersey: Prentice-Hall, 1961.

Chapman, Charles E. *A History of California: The Spanish Period.* New York, New York, 1921.

Cleland, Robert Glass. *A History of California: The American Period.* New York, New York, 1923.

Cleland, Robert Glass. *From Wilderness to Empire.* Alfred A. Knopf, 1944.

Cleland, Robert Glass. *The Cattle on a Thousand Hills: Southern California, 1850–80.* San Marino, California: The Henry E. Huntington Library and Art Gallery, 1941.

Coblentz, Edmond D. *William Randolph Hearst: A Portrait in His Own Words.* New York, New York: Simon and Schuster, 1952.

Coffman, Taylor. *Building for Hearst and Morgan: Voices from the George Loorz Papers.* Berkeley, California: Rev. ed. Berkeley Hills Books, 2003.

Cronin, William, George Miles and Jay Gitlin eds. *Under an Open Sky: Rethinking America's Western Past.* New York, New York: W.W. Norton & Co., 1992.

Dagget, Dan. *Beyond the Rangeland Conflict Toward a West that Works.* Good Steward Project, 2nd Edition, 2000.

Dale, Harrison Clifford. *The Ashley-Smith Explorations and the Discovery of a Central Route to the Pacific, 1822–1830.* Cleveland, Ohio, 1918.

Diamond, Henry L. and Patrick F. Noonan. *Land Use in America.* Washington, D.C.: Island Press, 1996.

Endicott, Eve. *Land Conservation Through Public/Private Partnerships.* Washington, D.C.: Island Press, 1993.

Englehardt, Rev. Zephyrin. *The Missions and Missionaries of California, Vol I.* San Francisco, California: The James H. Barry Co., 1908–1915.

Englehardt, Father Zephyrin. *The Missions and Missionaries of California, Vol. II.* Santa Barbara, California: Mission Santa Barbara, 1929.

Fink, Augusta. *Monterey: The Presence of the Past.* San Francisco, California. Chronicle Books, 1972.

Gessner, David. *All the Wild that Remains.* New York, New York. W.W. Norton Co, 2015.

Gibbs, Jocelyn and Nicholas Olsberg. Carefree *California: Cliff May and the Romance of the Ranch House.* New York, New York: Art, Design & Architecture Museum, University of California, Santa Barbara in association with Rizzoli International Publications, Inc., 2012.

Gidney, C.M., Benjamin Brooks, Edwin M. Sheridan. *History of Santa*

Barbara: San Luis Obispo and Ventura Counties California. Chicago, Illinois, 1917.

Hess, Alan, Alan Weintraub. *Rancho Deluxe: Rustic Dreams and Real Western Living*. San Francisco, California: Chronicle Books, 2000.

Hess, Alan. *The Ranch House*. New York, New York: Harry N. Abrams, Inc., 2004.

Hittell, Theodore H. *History of California, Vols 1-4*. San Francisco, California: N.J. Stone and Co., 1897.

Hough, Michael. *Out of Place: Restoring Identity to the Regional Landscape*. New Haven, Connecticut: Yale University Press, 1990.

Igler, David. *Cowboys: Miller & Lux and the Transformation of the Far West, 1850–1920*. Berkeley, California: University of California Press, 2001.

Jackson, Helen Hunt. *Glimpses of California and the Missions*. Boston, Massachusetts: Little Brown, 1903.
Jackson, Helen Hunt. *Ramona*. Boston, Massachusetts: Roberts Brothers, 1884.

Jurmain, Claudia, David Lavender and Larry L. Meyer. *Rancho Los Alamitos: Ever Changing, Always the Same*. Berkeley and Long Beach, California: Rancho Los Alamitos Foundation and Heyday, 2011.

Kastner, Victoria. *Hearst Castle: The Biography of a Country House*. New York, New York: Abrams, 2000.

Kastner, Victoria. *Hearst Ranch: Family, Land and Legacy*. New York, New York: Abrams, 2013.

Kastner, Victoria. *Hearst's San Simeon: The Gardens and the Land*. New York, New York: Abrams, 2009.

Keen, Jim with Amy Reeves. *Great Ranches of the West*. Colorado Springs, Colorado: KM Media, Inc., 2007.

Kirsch, Robert R., William S. Murphy. *West of the West: Witnesses to the California Experience, 1542–1906*. New York, New York: Dutton, 1967.

Marschner, Janice. *California: A Snapshot in Time 1850*. Sacramento, California: Coleman Ranch Press.

Morrow, William W. *Spanish and Mexican Private Land Grants*. San Francisco and Los Angeles, California, 1923.

Murray, Ken. *The Golden Days of San Simeon*. Garden City, New York: Doubleday, 1971.

Nadeau, Remi A. *City Makers: The Story of Southern California's First Boom, 1868–76*. Los Angeles, California: Trans-Anglo Books, 1965.

Nasaw, David. *The Chief: The Life of William Randolph Hearst*. New York, New York: Houghton Mifflin, 2000.

Older, Mr. and Mrs. Fremont. *George Hearst: California Pioneer*. Los Angeles, California: Westernlore, 1966.

Paul, Linda Leigh. *Ranches of the American West*. New York, New York: Rizzoli International Publications, Inc., 2009.

Pierce, Marjorie. *East of the Gablians*. Santa Cruz, California: Western Tanager Press/Valley Publishers, 1976.

Pincetl, Stephanie S. *Transforming California: A Political History of Land Use and Development*. Baltimore, Maryland: Johns Hopkins University Press, 1999.

Pitt, Leonard. *The Decline of the Californios: A Social History of the Spanish-Speaking Californians, 1846–1890*. Berkeley, California: University of California Press, 1998.

Poett, A. Dibblee. *Rancho San Julian*. Santa Barbara, California: Fithian Press, Santa Barbara Historical Society, 1991.

Pollan, Michael. *The Omnivore's Dilemma*. New York, New York: Penguin Press, 2006.

Prago, Albert. *The Revolutions in Spanish America*. New York, New York: Macmillan, 1970.

Price, B. Byron. *Imagining the Open Ranch*. Fort Worth, Texas: Amon Carter Museum, 1998.

Proctor, Ben. *William Randolph Hearst: The Early Years, 1863–1910*. New York, New York: Oxford University Press, 1998.

Robinson, Alfred. *Life in California*. New York, New York: Wiley and Putnam, 1846.

Robinson, Judith. *The Hearsts: An American Dynasty*. San Francisco, California: Telegraph Hill Press, 1991.

Robinson, W.W. *Land in California*. Berkeley, California: University of California Press, 1948.

Robinson, W.W. Ranchos Become Cities. Pasadena, California: San Pasqual Press, 1939.

Robinson, W.W. *The Forest and the People*. Los Angeles, California, 1946.

Salatin, Joel. *Salad Bar Beef*. Swoope, Virginia: Polyface, Inc., 1995.

Samon, Katherine Ann. *Ranch House Style*. New York, New York: Clarkson Potter/Publishers, 2003.

Savory, Allan. *Holistic Resource Management: A Model for a Healthy Planet*. 1988.

Savory, Allan, Jody Butterfield. *Holistic Management: A New Framework for Decision Making*. 1998.

Schacht, Henry M. and Shirl Woodson. *The California Cowboy*. Ketchum, Idaho: Stoecklein Publishing, 2000.

Sheridan, Sol N. *History of Ventura County*. Chicago, Illinois, 1926.

Smith, Burt. Intensive Grazing Management: Forage, Animals, Men, Profits.

Starr, Kevin. *Americans and the California Dream, 1850–1914*. New York, New York: Oxford Univeristy Press, 1973.

Starr, Kevin. *California: A History*. New York, New York: The Modern Library, 2007.

Starr, Kevin. *Endangered Dreams: The Great Depression in California*. New York, New York: Oxford University Press, 1996.

Starr, Kevin. *Material Dreams: Southern California Through the 1920s*. New York, New York: Oxford University Press, 1990.

Strain, Ethel H., Kathryn Hollister. *The Ancestors and Descendants of Albert G. Hollister*. Santa Barbara, California: W.T. Genns, Publisher, 1970.

Slavin, Neal. *When Two or More are Gathered Together*. New York, New York: Farrar, Straus and Giroux, 1976.

Stoecklein, David R. *Southern California Coastal Mountains to the Sea*. Newport Beach, California: The Irvine Company, LLC, 2011.

Swanberg, W.A. *Citizen Hearst: A Biography of William Randolph Hearst*. New York, New York: Scribner's, 1961.

Taliaferro, John. *Charles M. Russell: The Life and Legend of America's Cowboy Artist*. Boston, Massachusetts: Little, Brown, 1996.

Thomas, Tony. *Joel McCrea: A Film History*. Burbank, California: Riverwood Press and Frances Dee McCrea Trust, 2013.

Tompkins, Walker A. *King of the Sheep Barons: The Life and Times of Colonel W.W. Hollister* (unpublished manuscript), Santa Barbara Historical Society, 1960.

Tompkins, Walker A. *Santa Barbara's Royal Rancho*. Goleta, California: Dos Pueblos Publications, 1987.

Treadwell, Edward F. *The Cattle King*. Lafayette, California: Great West Books, 2005.

Vernon, Edward W. *Asistencia Santa Margarita de Cortona*. Santa Barbara, California: Viejo Press, 2012.

Ward, Nancy. *Hollister Ranch: Its History, Preservation and People*. Hollister Ranch Conservancy, 2004.

Weber, Msgr. Francis J. *Santa Margarita de Cortona Asistencia*. Anno Domini Publishing and the Saint Francis Historical Society, 2003.

Weingarten, David and Lucia Howard. *Ranch Houses: Living the California Dream*. New York, New York: Rizzoli Publishing, 2009.

Wheelwright, Jane Hollister. *The Ranch Papers: A California Memoir*. Santa Monica, California: The Lapis Press, 1988.

White, Richard D. *Will Rogers: A Political Life*. Lubbock, Texas: Texas Tech University Press, 2011.

Winslow, Carleton M., Jr., and Nickloa L. Frye. *The Enchanted Hill*. Hilbrae, California: Celestial Arts, 1980.

Worcester, Don. *Cowboy with a Camera: Erwin E. Smith, Cowboy Photographer*. Fort Worth, Texas: Amon Carter Museum.

Yagoda, Ben. *Will Rogers: A Biography*. Norman, Oklahoma: University of Oklahoma Press, 2000.

ARTICLES, ETC.:

Badger, K. Reka. "Hollister Ranch." *Santa Barbara Seasons Magazine*, Spring 2013.

"Dust of the Trail." *The Cattleman 13*, June 1926.

Hanc, John. "His Ranch is Everybody's (William S. Hart)." *New York Times*. November 1, 2015.

Historical Society of Southern California Quarterly, Fall 2015, Volume 97, No. 3. Oakland, California: University of California Press, 2015.

Howser, Huell. "Hearst Ranch—California's Gold." California Public Television Broadcast. September 7, 2009.

John Byers Papers. Architecture and Design Collection, Art, Design & Architecture Museum, University of California, Santa Barbara.

Kristof, Nicholas. "The (Fake) Meat Revolution." *New York Times*. September 20, 2015.

Mathes, Valerie Sherer. "Helen Hunt Jackson, Amelia Stone Quinton, and the Mission Indians of California." *Southern California Quarterly*, Summer 2014, Vol. 96, No. 2. Society of Southern California.

"Ranches in California." Memphis, Tennessee: Books LLC®, Wiki Series, 2011.

Santa Barbara Seasons Magazine, Spring 2013. Santa Barbara, California.

Santa Lucia Preserve, Volumes 1–4. Newport Beach, California: Club Resort Publishing.

Thomas, Steven M. "Tony Moiso: the Man and the Land." *OC Metro Register*. August 26, 2013.

True, Margo. "Dinner on a Dream Ranch" *Sunset Magazine*, December 2012.

Working Ranch Magazine. Multiple Issues. Van Nuys, California.

ACKNOWLEDGMENTS

We are first and foremost indebted to the many people who welcomed us to their properties, especially to those whose ranches comprise the heart and soul of this book. They are, in order:

Rancho Camulos: Susan Falck, Director, Rancho Camulos Museum.

Rancho Santa Margarita: Rob Rossi; Vicky Farley, Executive Assistant; Destini Cavalleto, Public Relations; Kathy Loftus, Santa Margarita Historical Society.

Rancho Los Alamitos: Pamela Seager, Executive Director; Claudia Jurmain, Director of Special Projects and Publications.

Rancho Cienega del Gabilan: Julie Baldocchi.

Hunewill Ranch: Betsy Hunewill Elliott.

Likely Land & Livestock: Athena and Bill Flournoy, Rodney Flournoy, Pearce Flournoy.

Five Dot Ranch: Tod and Loretta Swickard.

Piedra Blanca Ranch: Steve Hearst; Ben Higgins, Director of Agricultural Operations; Victoria Kastner, Publicity Director.

Tresch Ranch: Joe and Kathy Tresch.

Moore Ranch: Margaret and Jim Moore.

Rancho Canada Larga: Steve Gaggero.

Will Rogers Ranch: Jennifer Rogers; Jacob Krumwiede, Assistant Director; Trudi Sandmeier, Director, Graduate heritage Conservation Programs; Stephen Bylin, Sector Superintendent;

Lester Woods, Guide.

Beauty Ranch: Tjiska Van Wyk, Executive Director; Deborah Large, Community Events Manager.

Joel McCrea Ranch: Wyatt McCrea.

French Ranch: Joel Shukovsky.

Hollister Ranch: John McCarty, Co-op Manager; Kathi Carlson, Sue Benech Field, Co-op Volunteers.

Paicines Ranch: Sallie and Matt Calhoun; Leticia Hain, Event Center Manager.

Rancho San Carlos: Mike Kelly, Chief Operating Officer, Santa Lucia Preserve; Tom Gray, Founding Partner at Preserve Communities; Mark Miller, Historian; Ron Builta, Director of Property Operations.

Belcampo Farms: Anya Fernald, CEO; Laura Beaudrow, Assistant to CEO; Mark Klever, Former President; Mirari Romero, Former Executive Assistant.

Thanks are also due to those who added greatly to our experience and perspective, even though, in some cases, their ranches were not able to be included:

Dennis and Sandy Ahearn, Steve and Debbie Arnold, Rachel Barnes, Margi Bertram, Ellen Calomiris, California Cattleman's Association, Mark Chaconas, Pam and Dan Dorian, Leslie and Steve Dorrance, Molly Dorrance, Devere and Laura Dressler, Sandy and Justin Faggioli, Terry Guidetti, Paul Grafton, Juanell and Dave Hepburn, Lauren Benward Krause, John and Dee Lacey, Christine and Jim Maguire, Marin Agricultural Land Trust, Wendy Millet, Joe & Julie Morris, Polly Osborne, Will Pennebaker, James Poett, Patricia Pope, Claud Pritchard, Linda and Jack Russ, Sherry and Carson Scheller, Henry Schulte, Steve Sinton, Barbara and Bill Spencer, Tom Steyer and Kat Taylor, Jason Switzer, Mark Switzer, Richard Thieriot, Marissa Thornton, Daryl Twisselman, Jack Varian, John Varian, Dwayne Waddell, Marina Washburn, Paul Wiseman, George and Elaine Work.

Several friends were valuable resources or lent expert advice: Riley Bechtel, Dave Brigantino, Jill Cohen, Pat and Nancy Forster, Daniel P. Gregory, Mary Kennedy, Joanna Kerns, Arthur E. Nicholas, Jack and Zan Peat, Elisa Stancil and Chuck Levine, and Suzanne Tucker.

Peta Rimington was an early and enthusiastic supporter and collaborator, introducing us to numerous contacts and accompanying the author on some of his excursions. If we had an angel on our shoulder during this journey, it was Peta.

Throughout the project Melissa Kamen provided unstinting and patient assistance in the research and writing, and Matt Walla expertise in fine tuning the photographic material.

This book would not have happened without the vision and commitment of our publisher, Rizzoli International Publications, especially its Vice President Charles Miers, and our editor and designer Douglas Curran.

Melba Levick expresses immense gratitude to her husband and partner, Hugh Levick, for his unfailing assistance on this book and for the pleasure of having the rich experience of the discovery of the California ranches.

Marc Appleton is indebted to his parents, Frank and Ariel Appleton, and the Brooks Family, who early on nurtured his respect for the land and his appreciation for those whose lives are affected daily by its blessings and its curses.

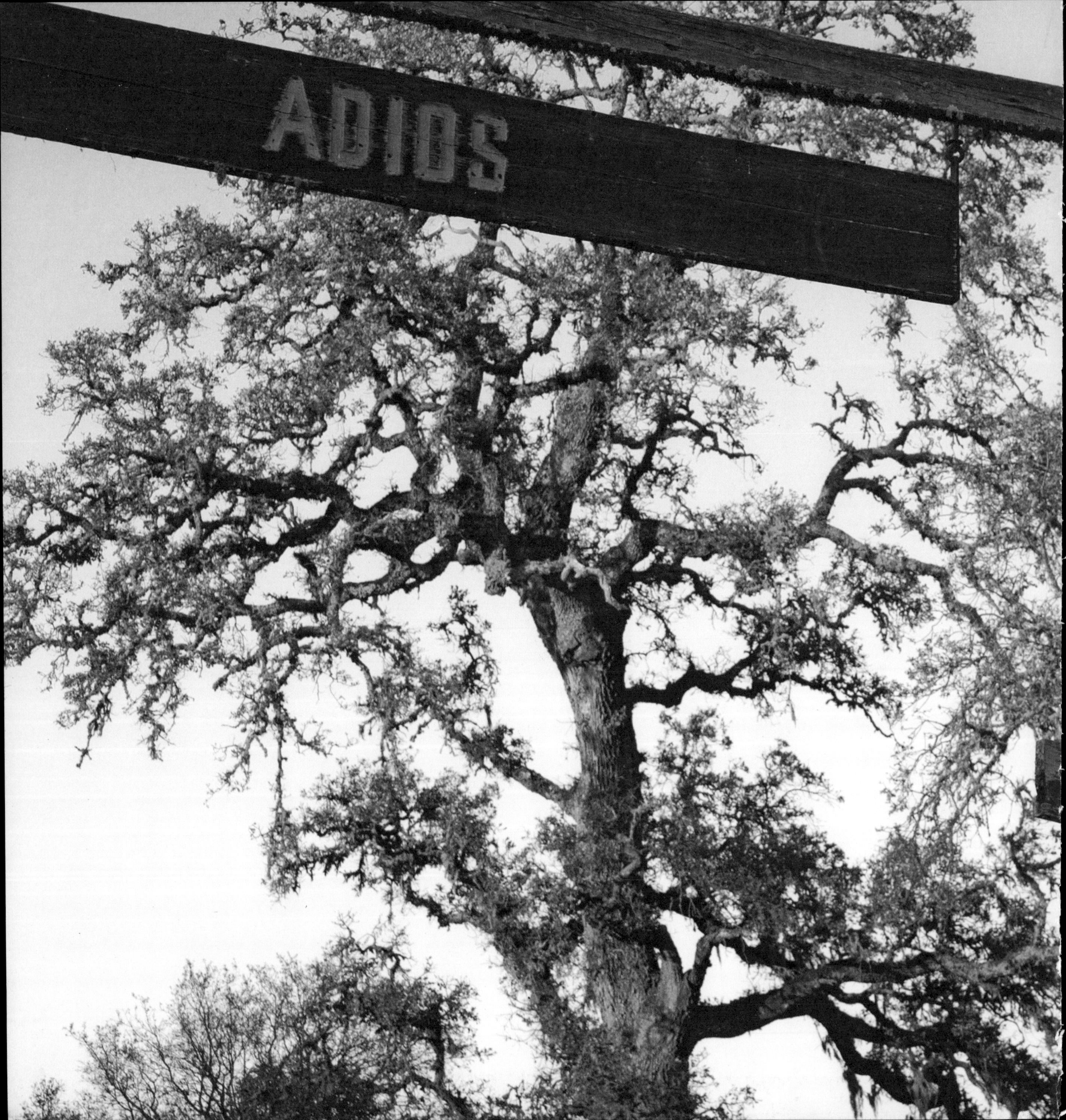
ADIOS